WALK
HISTORIC HALIFAX

GRANT MACLEAN

NIMBUS
PUBLISHING LTD

Nimbus Publishing Limited
P.O. Box 9301, Station A
Halifax, NS   B3K 5N5
(902)455-4286

Design: Kathy Kaulbach
Printed and bound in Canada

Canadian Cataloguing in Publication Data
MacLean, Grant.
Walk historic Halifax
Includes bibliographical references.
ISBN 1-55109-135-6

1. Halifax (N.S.)—Tours. 2. Halifax (N.S.)—History. 3. Walking—
Nova Scotia—Halifax—Guidebooks. 4. Historic sites—Nova Scotia—
Halifax—Guidebooks. I. Title.
FC2346.18.M33 1996   917.16'225044   C96-950055-6
F1039.5.H17M33 1996

Photo credits: Archives du Séminaire de Québec pp. 98, 167; Charles P. deVolpi Collection, Special Collections, Dalhousie University pp. 25, 47, 59, 72, 91, 124, 131, 135, 143, 159; *Illustrated Encyclopedia of Ships, Boats, Vessels and Other Water-borne Craft* pp. 104; J. J. Stewart Collection, Special Collections, Dalhousie University pp. 8, 40; L. B. Jenson pp. 56, 145, 155; National Archives of Canada pp. 29, 108, 113, 118; Nova Scotia Museum pp. 129; Parks Canada pp. 79, 80, 81, 86; Public Archives of Nova Scotia pp. iv, 5, 6, 10, 11, 49, 63, 106, 178; Public Records Office pp. 73, 113, 118, 172; Shambala Centre pp. 151; Special Collections, Dalhousie University pp. 2, 95; William Inglis Morse Collection, Special Collections, Dalhousie University pp. 54, 122, 164.

Contents

HMS *Shannon* leading her prize the American frigate *Chesapeake* into Halifax harbour, 1813 (Schetky/King, 1830).

Acknowledgements

A book—even a small one—owes its existence to many sources and inspirations. Thomas Raddall's popular histories, in particular his enduring *Halifax: Warden of the North;* Elizabeth Pacey's richly evocative portrayals of the historic city; the late Harry Piers' scholarly work on the evolution of the fortress system; and Dr. Louis Collins's *In Halifax Town,* along with his warmly described and erudite walking tours—these have kindled and fanned a flame of appreciation for the city's past as well as providing a wealth of original material, which this guide has freely drawn upon.

Many people have given generous technical help. I am grateful to Ron McDonald and Glenn Lush at the Citadel, Garry Shutlak and Margaret Campbell at the Public Archives of Nova Scotia, Ruth Whitehead and Dr. Marie Ellwood at the Nova Scotia Museum, Marilyn Smith at the Maritime Command Museum, and Karen Smith at the Killam Library, Dalhousie University. I would like to express thanks to Alan Doyle of Nova Scotia Tourism, who read the manuscript and offered helpful advice and encouragement; to Emily Sell, who edited the piece; to David Brown, who produced the handsome maps and who was a stalwart friend throughout; to Sherian Underwood, whose idea this book was; and to James Gimian, a warrior in the old fashion, who along with other friends offered inspiration, energy, and support. Any failures of vision or of textual or historical accuracy rest entirely with the author.

Grant MacLean
Halifax, Nova Scotia
March 1996

To: My Gail,
Allen Doyle

Preface

This is a guide for people who want to explore historic Halifax, a city made for pleasant and captivating walks.

Halifax has an extraordinary past. There can be few other cities of its age or size which have seen so much colour, spectacle, triumph, and heartache—or which have played so illustrious a part on the world's stage. It was a role that was often cast in the momentous military adventures of the British Empire, but the city has also been eminent in politics, trade, industry, and education.

Situated on a peninsula that juts into a superb harbour, Halifax offers, along with its many historical points of interest, a variety of scenic excursions by land or sea. A tour of the old imperial forts will, for example, bring the explorer to delightful woodland walks and panoramic seascapes well suited to wandering, picnicking, simply enjoying nature—or for contemplating some of the vast currents of history that have swept through this old port.

Using Your Guide

The guide provides seven walking tours of the city, its fortress, and the surroundings. If you have the time before setting out, read the Introduction, which aims to give you a richer sense of the features covered in the tours. Then choose a tour route from the following Tour Highlights. Note that five of the tours—the Old Town, Citadel Hill, South End, McNabs Island, and the first segment of the North End tours—start within easy walking distance of the downtown area. The other starting points—Point Pleasant Park, York Redoubt, and the extended segments of the North End tour—can be reached by car or bus.

Tour Highlights

The major sights of Halifax are divided into seven tours. Each tour's highlights are described below, with the general area of each tour shown on the map opposite.

Tour 1 The Old Town (page 40):

Grand Parade—St. Paul's Church—Old Burying Ground—Government House—Old Brewery—Province House—Maritime Museum of the Atlantic—HMCS *Sackville*—Historic Properties. Optional short tour. (Walk.)

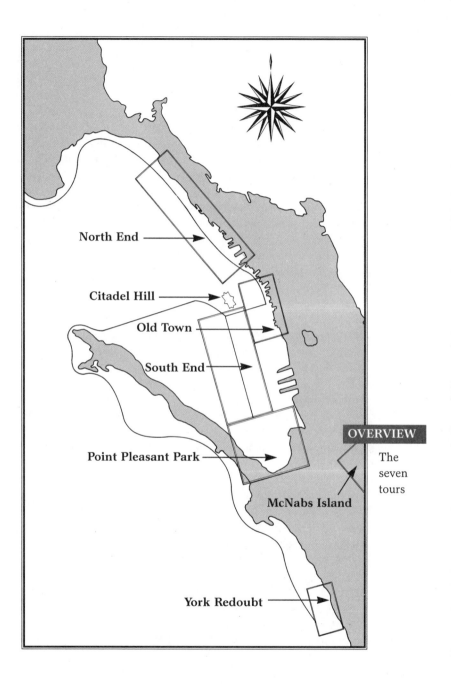

North End

Citadel Hill

Old Town

South End

Point Pleasant Park

McNabs Island

York Redoubt

OVERVIEW

The
seven
tours

Tour 2   Citadel Hill (page 72):

Historic panorama of the city—Old Town Clock—early nine-teenth-century fort—pageantry of Royal Artillery and 78th Highlanders—various displays, including "Tides of History" audiovisual show—Army Museum. (Walk.)

Tour 3   Point Pleasant Park (page 91):

Woodland and seaside walks, fine views of Northwest Arm and harbour channel—eighteenth-century Prince of Wales Martello Tower and other old fortifications. (Walk/Drive/Bus to park.)

Tour 4   York Redoubt via the Northwest Arm (page 108):

Impressive vistas of harbour entrance and McNabs Island—Northwest Arm—eighteenth- and nineteenth-century fort—World War II Fire Command Post display—woodland and cove side walks. (Drive/Bus to fort.)

Tour 5   North End and Beyond (page 122):

Brunswick Street (Walk)—Naval Dockyard—Maritime Command Museum—Halifax Explosion site. Optional extended tour: *Titanic* memorial cemetery—Bedford Basin—Prince's Lodge rotunda (Drive/Bus.)

Tour 6   South End (page 145):

Royal Artillery Park—Georgian homes—Fort Massey and Holy Cross Cemeteries—Public Gardens—Camp Hill—Nova Scotia Museum—additional points of interest including universities. (Walk.)

Tour 7   McNabs Island (page 164):

Island wilderness at harbour mouth—boat trip with views of har-bour and Georges Island—island walks—plants and wildlife—pic-nicking—Mauger Beach—Fort McNab and Ives Point Battery. (Ferry to island.)

Each tour is accompanied by a map of the area covered. Although most of the tours can be completed in as little as one hour, you may—depending on your interests—want to allow more time for exploration. The exception is the McNabs Island tour, which requires a minimum of about two and a half hours.

Combining Tours

Historic Halifax offers a variety of possible tours to satisfy your interests in the time you have available. Here are some suggestions for combining tours:

Half-Day Tour:
1. The Old Town (Tour 1-Short Tour).
2. Citadel Hill (Tour 2). If touring in the morning, be sure to be at the Citadel for the firing of the Noon Gun.

Full-Day Tour:
1. Morning: The Old Town and Citadel Hill (see above).
2. Afternoon: Point Pleasant Park (Tour 3) via the Public Gardens, or York Redoubt (Tour 4).

The Fortress:
1. Citadel Hill (Tour 2).
2. Point Pleasant Park (Tour 3).
3. York Redoubt (Tour 4).
4. McNabs Island (Tour 7).

Georgian and Victorian Halifax:
1. The Old Town (Tour 1).
2. North End (Tour 5).
3. South End (Tour 6).

Seashore Walks and Harbour Views:
1. Point Pleasant Park (Tour 3).
2. York Redoubt (Tour 4), including Northwest Arm.
3. McNabs Island (Tour 7).

Glimpses of Historic Halifax

Halifax has led the way in a variety of accomplishments, "firsts" and "oldests." It has the finest original Victorian public gardens in North America; the finest Georgian building in Canada (Province House); the Chief British imperial fortress in the Western Hemisphere; and the highest ratio of educational institutions to population in North America (five universities, two colleges).

First
- newspaper in Canada (*Halifax Gazette,* 1752)
- public gardens in Canada (1753)
- post office in Canada (1755)
- Board of Trade in Canada (1758)
- Legislative Assembly in Canada (1758)
- Martello tower in the British Empire (Prince of Wales Tower, 1798)
- yacht club in North America (1837)
- mail steamer to cross the Atlantic (Samuel Cunard's *Britannia,* 1840)
- Responsible Government—government by the people—in the British Empire (1848)
- covered skating rink in North America (1863)

Oldest
- Protestant Church in Canada (St. Paul's Church, 1750)
- operating saltwater ferry service in North America (1752)
- Lutheran church in Canada (Little Dutch Church, 1756)
- naval dockyard in North America (1759)
- English-speaking university in Canada and the overseas Empire (University of King's College, 1789)
- continuously occupied executive mansion in Canada (Government House, 1800)
- garrison library in Canada (Cambridge Library, 1817)
- most historic Parliament building in Canada (Province House, 1819)

Historic Sites and Institutions

The following is a list of National Historic Sites, museums, galleries, archives, and universities in Halifax. The numbers in parentheses indicate the tour in which the point of interest is described—for example, Nova Scotia Museum (6) indicates that the museum is described in Tour 6 (South End).

National Historic Sites:
Admiralty House, CFB Stadacona, Gottingen Street (5)
The Citadel, Citadel Hill (2)
Prince of Wales Martello Tower, Point Pleasant Park (3)
York Redoubt, Purcell's Cove Road (4)

Museums:

Army Museum, The Citadel (2)
Maritime Command Museum, Gottingen Street (5)
Maritime Museum of the Atlantic, 1675 Lower Water Street (1)
Nova Scotia Museum, 1747 Summer Street (6)
Thomas McCulloch Museum, Life Sciences Centre, Dalhousie
University (6)

Galleries:

Art Gallery of Nova Scotia, 1741 Hollis Street (1)
Dalhousie Art Gallery, 6101 University Avenue (6)
Mount Saint Vincent Gallery, 166 Bedford Highway (5)
St. Mary's Gallery, 593 Robie Street (6)

Archives:

Public Archives of Nova Scotia, 6016 University Avenue (6)
Maritime Command Museum Archives, Gottingen Street (5)
Dalhousie University Archives, Killam Memorial Library (6)
University of King's College Archives, 6350 Coburg Road (6)

Universities:

University of King's College, Coburg Road (6)
Dalhousie University, University Avenue (6)
St. Mary's University, Robie Street (6)
Mount Saint Vincent University, Bedford Highway (5)
Technical University of Nova Scotia, Barrington Street (1)

Halifax In History

Halifax is a pleasant, almost contented, city. Surrounded by the sea, its homes of long-gone merchants, sailors, and soldiers cluster up to the great fort on the hill, while its citizens go unhurriedly about their business and ships make their measured way into the harbour, as they have done for centuries. Sometimes only the boom of the midday gun or the whoops of nighttime revellers disturb the old seaport's calm.

It was not always so. From its birth in the eighteenth century, Halifax was swept by history's great waves, which occasionally brought prosperity but more often battered and warped the town's foundations. Halifax underwent extremes of human experience— pageantry and squalor, triumph and despair, tragedy and valour.

View of Halifax from Dartmouth Cove (Bouchette, 1832).

For Halifax was a British imperial bastion, caught up in the adventures of history's largest—some would say greatest— Empire. As a powerful military and naval base, in the eighteenth century it was the launching pad for the conquest of Canada; in the nineteenth century it became the new country's defensive strongpoint; and in this century's vast conflicts it was the lifeline for the mother country—at times the most important port in the world. During the age of sail, the era of "wooden ships and iron men," Halifax became a maritime powerhouse, only to find itself pioneering the steamships that snuffed out that age. It also took a trailblazing role in the Empire's political evolution as native sons pushed wide-ranging democratic reforms through the town's legislatures. Meanwhile, in the calms and eddies grew a robust civil society, with its distinguished universities, fine parks and gardens, and elegant homes.

The modern world has erased much of the past, yet much remains. Through the efforts of concerned people, in and around the city Georgian and Victorian buildings have been lovingly preserved, ancient forts renovated and re-garrisoned with highly drilled volunteers, and time-honoured traditions upheld. All the while, memories and echoes crowd in across the water, up the old streets, and around the dank walls of the fortress, coming to life in the very contours of the harbour, the patterns of its islands, and the ruling presence of the sea.

....

On Nova Scotia's Atlantic shore is a deep indentation forming a magnificent harbour. The Micmac, one of North America's indigenous peoples, called it *Kjipuktuk* ("at the great harbour"), from which the Europeans came to call it Chebucto. In the early 1600s Samuel de Champlain, explorer and founder of French Canada, noted the harbour as *fort saine*—"good and safe." When the first British officers saw it, they reported to London that it was the finest harbour they had ever seen.

It is easy to understand the praise. The inner harbour— Bedford Basin—is deep and, as one eighteenth-century sailor described it, large enough to hold the entire English navy. The harbour mouth is dominated on the one side by McNabs Island, on the other by the foot of the peninsula, and—further out—by tall granite bluffs. Forts placed on these points would command all access to the harbour.

At Nova Scotia's midpoint, the harbour is also wonderfully situated. From it, a naval power could control both the North American sea lanes and the land routes to the interior of Canada. As a port for mercantile trade, it was "as if nature had raised her up in the ocean as a vast pier for the fleets of the Atlantic."

This glittering prize was acquired at great cost. Once obtained, the harbour, the city of Halifax, and the fortress that burgeoned around them, for two centuries played a leading role in the expansion and defence of the British Empire—in the end, they were crucial to its very survival.

Race for an Empire

Halifax was born in the searing race for an empire.

Through much of the eighteenth century, Great Britain and France had vied for domination in Europe, on the high seas, and through their colonial possessions. By the 1740s Britain's foothold in her American colonies looked secure, but in Canada, France had built powerful fortresses at Quebec and Louisbourg.

The American colonists were especially worried by Louisbourg. Using this Cape Breton fortress as a base, French privateers preyed on their shipping and were taking some fat prizes; and there was the possibility of French military expeditions against New England ports and towns. So, in 1744, when war flared up again between Britain and France, Governor Shirley of Massachusetts organized an army of New England townspeople. By a combination of daring and determination—and with the assistance of luck and the Royal Navy—this force captured the mighty fortress of Louisbourg.

This feat of arms by a half-disciplined and often drunken, irregular army stunned the Western world. The French, for their part, were outraged and planned an expedition to recapture their fortress. A formidable fleet of over seventy warships—already assembled to support Bonnie Prince Charlie in his defeated invasion of England under the Duc D'Anville—was to use the harbour at Chebucto as a base and having taken Louisbourg, would then embark on a campaign to destroy English outposts. The tour de force was to be the burning of Boston.

As if the fates were against it, the great fleet was shattered by storm, wreck, and disease, and barely half the ships limped into Chebucto harbour. Their misfortune was not over: a few days after landing, D'Anville was dead (the officers said of apoplexy, the men said by poison), and his vice-admiral had thrown himself on his sword, leaving hundreds of their men to die of scurvy and smallpox on the shores of Bedford Basin. The survivors struggled home to France.

With cruel irony, only a year or so after this tragedy Louisbourg was handed back to the French as part of a peace treaty with England. The New Englanders were enraged. Not only were the blood and treasure they had expended in the capture of the fortress wasted, but the French menace was back in place, stronger than ever and with all damage made good by His Majesty's Government.

Governor Shirley demanded that an armed settlement be built to counterbalance Louisbourg and protect the New England colonies. This settlement, he said, must be situated at Chebucto harbour.

The Great Expedition

Shocked by the colonial anger and realizing the wisdom of Shirley's proposal, the British government moved with splendid efficiency to equip an expedition. Lord Halifax, as President of the Board of Trade and Plantations, produced a plan, and an advertisement was placed in the *London Gazette* calling for settlers for the new colony.

But in the rush to get the expedition under way, very few of the preferred type of settler—"officers and private men lately dismissed from H. M. land and sea service" and skilled craftsmen—arrived on board. The poor of London, however, saw their opportunity and flocked onto the ships, enticed by His Majesty's promise of free victuals and lodging. This was soon to have a harsh outcome.

No expense was spared to ensure that Great Britain would successfully acquire her new strongpoint: the expedition was lavishly equipped with everything from trinkets for the Indians to new-fangled "ventilators" to supply fresh air to the cramped settlers below deck. It was led by Colonel Edward Cornwallis, an incorruptible military bachelor, who on June 21, 1749, guided thirteen ships and three thousand settlers into Chebucto harbour, having enjoyed the smoothest of crossings.

Governor Edward Cornwallis (Chalmers, 1755).

The planners quickly laid out the town. At the centre was a Grand Parade for troop musterings, surrounded by a neat gridwork of streets named for the leading British statesmen and aristocrats of the day. Cornwallis named the town itself for the President of the Board of Trade and Plantations, using his title, Lord Halifax, rather than his name, Dunk.

Cornwallis's greatest concern was the town's defence—the French and their Micmac allies would not likely allow the new

British settlement much peace. Finding a garrison was easy: the British troops who had been occupying Louisbourg were simply shipped to Halifax, using the same vessels that had just landed the settlers. But the town still needed fortifications, physical barriers against attacks coming out of the wooded wilderness.

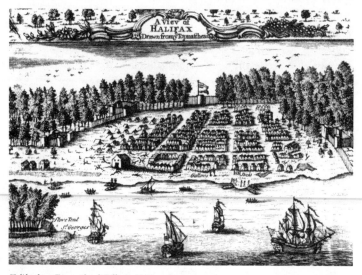

Halifax from Topmasthead (Jeffreys, 1750).

The captain-general now ran into his first real obstacle: many of the new colonists simply refused to work. Drunken and undisciplined, nonchalant about the Indian threat, and ignorant of the rigours of the Nova Scotian winter, only when the first news of Indian scalpings arrived did the work speed up. Gradually the town was built, and with it the defences—a series of small wooden forts connected by a log palisade.

When winter arrived, the results of the settlers' indiscipline became terribly clear. Not enough shelter had been built and large numbers of settlers—dirty, packed tightly together on the ships and in what housing there was—died from disease. When the weather broke most of the survivors wandered off to the less challenging climate in New England.

After the first terrible winter, prospects improved. New Englanders soon arrived in large numbers, seeing good profits to be made from His Majesty's bounty. Meanwhile, the Lords of Trade arranged to send more energetic and able people from

Europe, and in the next several years hundreds of Rhinelanders and a good number of Huguenots arrived. Within a few years large sums of money were being made by enterprising local merchants, who fitted out schooners with what weapons could be obtained. The schooners, acting as privateers, harried French shipping in the latest war between the two nations.

Garrison Town

In 1758 over twelve thousand naval and military men, under the command of Admiral Boscawen and General Amherst, flooded into Halifax, bent on the final destruction of Louisbourg. The influx transformed the small and shabby town in a way that was repeated often over the next two centuries. The narrow streets were filled with military men and martial airs, the harbour lay covered with a forest of Royal Navy ships, while merchants with the proper connections made fortunes supplying provisions to the services.

Rum shops, taverns, and brothels sprang to life, charging out-rageous prices and with little chance of meeting the demand. The town was developing a reputation. As one observer put it—only partly exaggerating—"the business of one half the town is to sell rum and the other half to drink it." The rough clamour of sailors, redcoats, and tars surged through the streets. To keep some sort of order the civil authorities periodically held public hangings on the waterfront and on George Street, while the military dis-patched their troublemakers with musket fire on the Common.

And then the party was over. Filling the harbour with their sails, the 160 ships of the fleet carried the general and his army to Louisbourg. After a muddled campaign the fortress fell and was utterly demolished, with much of the stone (originally carried from Normandy) finding its way into buildings going up in the town. Halifax now lay unchallenged astride the route into Canada.

The following year General Wolfe set out from his base at Halifax on his audacious campaign to conquer Quebec. After that fortress's capture, France's dreams for her North American empire died. With their allies expelled from the continent, the Micmac made peace with the British and buried the hatchet at Halifax. British North America was now secure. His Majesty's investment in Halifax had been handsomely repaid.

But with the arrival of peace, a bleak pattern emerged: it grad-ually dawned on the town that the authorities viewed Halifax as a weapon of war and little else—in peacetime, the town and its fortifications were neglected. To make things worse, it also became clear that the townspeople were seen by the military almost as interlopers, as just useless mouths to feed in the event of a siege.

Resentment grew. It was directed at the garrison, at its morals—the drinking dens and bawdy-houses in the upper streets of the town built their trade on the troops' need for off-duty diversions—and at the heavy imperial hand of the Governor. The grumblings became sharper when, in 1765, the British tried to impose the Stamp Act: Haligonians raised a gibbet on Citadel Hill to hang local officials in effigy.

Further south the outcry was louder still and the Halifax garrison departed for Boston to support the redcoats struggling to control the situation. After the defeats at Lexington and Bunker Hill, in the decisive year of 1776 General Howe withdrew from Boston and landed in Halifax, with his bloodied and surly army, to plan the next move in the campaign against the rebellious American colonies. As before, the streets swarmed with fighting men: redcoats, sailors of the fleet, Hessians in their blue coats, and a full brigade of Highlanders; as before, the town's fabric was distorted by the influx of sudden wealth and by "King Rum" and bawdy-houses, all mixed in with the harsh trade of press gangs and privateers. This time, though, the town had a rougher ordeal as defeated men took out their bitterness on all and sundry.

....

The Governor's House, Mather's and St. Paul's churches (Short, 1759).

So it must have been with even greater mixed feelings than usual that townspeople watched the army leave for its attack on New York; Howe took all available troops with him, leaving the town defenceless. Throughout the war a question hung in the air: Would Nova Scotians join the rebellion against British rule? After all, the colony had sent four delegates to the Continental Congress in Philadelphia, while most Haligonians were of New England descent and had close ties with the older colonies.

But the uprising never really caught fire. In the first place, as George Washington himself regretfully said, troops could not be spared to assist it; then there were often British troops in Halifax that discouraged rash acts; and as the war progressed, large numbers of Loyalists arrived in the town, swelling the anti-revolutionary sentiment. Among them were many black Loyalists—the first of many refugees of African heritage from the United States—who also began to scratch out a precarious existence in the overstretched colony labelled by the new arrivals "Nova Scarcity."

After the British surrender at Yorktown, Halifax stood alone as the last base in North America of the British Army and the Royal Navy. Had Nova Scotia too rebelled, the Union Jack would have gone home with His Majesty's forces and with it the dream of Canada as a separate nation.

Sons of the King

For much of the next century the United States of America was the chief concern of His Majesty's strategists. When would the new nation launch itself at British North America and drive the despised monarchists off the mainland forever? In this standoff, Halifax found itself at the centre of calculations.

In the meantime, the town got on with business—and pleasure. The first of many royal guests arrived in 1786 in the person of Prince William, one of George III's dissipated sons. Accompanied by a gilded coterie of officers, he led a debauched existence, and the parties held then became part of the town's legends. (At one typical regimental dinner, twenty guests drank sixty-three bottles of wine.)

One of the prince's companions during his stay was Frances Wentworth, the lovely and ambitious wife of the former Governor of New Hampshire, Sir John Wentworth, the most prominent of the American Loyalist refugees. When Sir John became lieutenant governor of Nova Scotia in 1792, town gossips

THE WENTWORTHS' BALL

*I*n 1792 an enraptured town reporter described the year's great event—the Governor and his lady's grand ball and supper at the old Government House on Hollis Street:

"The company being assembled in the Levee Room at eight o'clock, the band played God Save the King, three times over, after which the country dances commenced, two sets dancing at the same time. The whole house was open, every room illuminated and elegantly decorated. There was a room set apart for cotillions above-stairs for those who chose to dance them, and a band provided on purpose. During the dancing there were refreshments of ice, orgeat, capillaire, and a variety of other things. The ladies sat down at table and the gentlemen waited on them....

Lady Frances Wentworth (c 1769).

The viands and wines were delectable, and mirth, grace and good humour seemed to have joined hands to grace some glorious festival. But this was only for the friends of the Governor and lady. When the ladies left the supper room the gentlemen sat down at table, when the Governor gave toasts with 'three times three,' and an applicable tune was played after each bumper, which had an admirable effect. At two o'clock the dancing recommenced and at four the company retired."

had a field day—there was little doubt that Frances's friends in high places had pulled some of the right strings. After Prince William's departure, the Wentworths pushed ahead with their life of extravagant gaiety, soon to find an energetic companion in another of the King's offspring when Prince Edward arrived in Halifax with his mistress, the darkly beautiful Julie St. Laurent.

The prince made a brilliant and lasting impression on the shabby town, bluntly signalling his ambitions by decrying the "miserable state of all the Works and Public buildings." For, in contrast to his brothers, Edward, trained in the Prussian school, was an energetic and highly conscientious military man.

During Edward's stay the grinding series of Napoleonic Wars began. He was convinced that the French would pour across the Atlantic, capture Halifax and go on to retake Canada; and as Commander-in-Chief of His Majesty's forces in Nova Scotia, he set about improving the fortifications and ruthlessly tightening up garrison discipline. The innovation of which he was most proud was a "telegraph" system for sending military messages by means of visual signals; keeping duty and pleasure in fine balance, he used the system to keep in touch with his command from the lodge he shared with Mlle. St. Laurent on the shore of Bedford Basin (henceforth known as Prince's Lodge).

As the glittering round of parties, dinners, and balls swirled on, so did the erection of new public buildings and fortifications, all designed to make the town a worthy headquarters for a Prince of the Realm. Edward planned the Town Clock, for almost two centuries Halifax's best-known landmark, and saw to the building of the beautiful St. George's Church. The boom did not proceed without obstacle: The Board of Ordnance initially refused to fund the Prince of Wales Tower on Point Pleasant (Edward had impetuously gone ahead without permission), and in his turn, Governor Wentworth ran into trouble with the Nova Scotia legislature over the huge costs for the new Government House. But in the end the town benefited from these

Prince
Edward,
Duke of Kent.

fine buildings and several others redolent of the age.

With the Prince's departure in 1800, a memorable period in the town's history came to an end; well into the new century it was referred to nostalgically as "the Duke's time." Edward, as Duke of Kent, went on to find a secure niche in history: After a sad separation from Mlle. St. Laurent, he dutifully took a wife and fathered the future Queen Victoria.

Washington and Waterloo

As before in times of war, privateers and press gangs did a fine trade in Halifax. Booty taken from French ships was stored and sold on Water Street, while captured French seamen were imprisoned in the town or on Melville Island. Naval press gangs—often flouting the terms of warrants worked out with the town authorities—beat up able-bodied townsmen or farmers and dragged them off to the shackles of service in the King's ships. Those who could not be flogged into submission were executed and then—coated in tar to keep off the crows—hung from gibbets on Mauger Beach.

While this gallantry was going on in the name of the Empire, the American threat suddenly became real when, in 1812, President Madison sent troops over the border into Upper Canada, and New England privateers attacked British shipping in the Atlantic. In Halifax, the military hurriedly put the fortress in order while British forces from the garrison captured eastern Maine. During the occupation they levied taxes, carrying off a sizeable sum, which was later to be donated to the town as the Castine Fund. A procession of captured Americans arrived to join the French prisoners in and around the town.

The Halifax fortress's outermost line of defence was always the storm-beaten ships of the Royal Navy, cruising far out in the Atlantic. So Haligonians were appalled when the navy was handed a series of defeats by the larger and more heavily gunned United States frigates. Then, in a straight fight off Boston between HMS *Shannon* and the United States frigate *Chesapeake,* the British ship won a quick and bloody victory. All Halifax turned out to cheer from the harbour side as *Shannon*—under the command of the young Provo Wallis, a native son—led the American vessel into captivity. At the Old Burying Ground three hundred redcoats fired a salute as the slain American captain was laid to rest.

As the war ground on, Britain gradually built up military strength at her base in Halifax, launching attacks from it in 1814, which culminated in the burning of Washington. General Ross, the commander of the British forces, was killed shortly afterwards. He, in his turn, was buried in the town cemetery.

In 1815 the Duke of Wellington defeated Napoleon at Waterloo, and Great Britain's signing of peace agreements with both France and the United States made it a momentous year. For the next century there was no major threat to the Empire.

The imperial defenders felt a need to keep up their guard if peace was to be secure. They had finally realized that it made little sense to let the fortress at Halifax decay in peacetime, only to spend huge amounts of money to bring it into order when there was a threat. Starting in 1829, when work on the current Citadel began, the Royal Engineers spent the nineteenth century building new and more solid defences, renovating the old ones, and supplying the lot with ever more powerful weaponry.

Pax Britannica

For fifty-five years—from the accession of George III to the Battle of Waterloo—Britain had been almost constantly at war, and for two out of every three years of its existence, Halifax had been embroiled in the drive and clamour of British war expeditions. With the advent of lasting peace, the town could turn to more mundane concerns.

Once again, after the bulk of the naval and military forces sailed away, a depression hit the town. The slump deepened with the abolition of slavery in the British West Indies, where the old exploitative system for the mass production of rum, sugar, and molasses could not be maintained. A flood of destitute English, Irish, Scots, and Welsh escaping the postwar depression in the mother country did not help economic conditions; while many moved on into the Canadian interior, many others settled in the town and in the colony.

There was, nevertheless, money available for worthy projects. A bemedalled veteran of Waterloo, the Earl of Dalhousie, set about the development of inland trade and along the way created the university that bears his name, using money brought back from Maine in the War of 1812.

As the century unfolded, there were empire-shaking political developments in the town. As early as 1758 Nova Scotia had

SAM SLICK OF SLICKVILLE

In 1835 a series of satirical sketches about Sam Slick, a "genuine Yankee" peddler of clocks appeared in Howe's *Novascotian*. Later published as *The Clockmaker*, they became a literary sensation, particularly in England, where the parody of American manners and attitudes was found to be most amusing.

The author was Thomas C. Haliburton, "the father of American humour," a friend of Joseph Howe, a loyal Tory, and the Chief Justice of the Court of Common Pleas of Nova Scotia. Sam Slick ("of Slickville in Connecticut") was an entertaining character and much of his humour has weathered well. But the judge also had an agenda in mind, using the figure of the clock peddler to aim his barbs at a variety of targets.

Foremost of these was the democratic brashness, "calculatin'" shrewdness, and massive assurance of the young republic to the south. As an American, Sam was proud that his horse could pass all others on the Nova Scotian roads and of his own cleverness in selling brass clocks (marked up from $6.50 to $40) to the locals. He lost no chance to tweak the British Lion's tail: the King of England would be no match as an orator for Daniel Webster, who would "talk him out of sight in half an hour." As for the average American:

"He's the chap that has both speed, wind and bottom; he's clear grit—ginger to the backbone, you may depend. It's generally allowed there ain't the beat of them to be found anywhere. Spry as a fox, supple as an eel, and cute as a weasel ... they fairly take the shine off creation; they are actilly equal to cash."

Haliburton, through the peddler, also took some hefty swipes at the imperial British and their colonial policy, which he was coming to see as unwise and poorly informed. Sam found the British nickname "John Bull" well chosen: "they are all bull-necked, bull-headed folks ... a-pawin' and a-roarin' the whole time ... as headstrong as mules, and as conceited as peacocks."

Sam had some sharp observations about Nova Scotia and its chief town, and here, too, Haliburton had clear targets in mind. He especially wanted to throw his weight behind the building of a railroad to open up the colony for trade. He also wanted to arouse his countrymen from sleepiness, as he saw it, and awake them to their colony's potential.

To Sam, in the colony there was "neither spirit, enterprise nor patriotism ... the whole country is as inactive as a bear in winter that does nothing but scrouch up in his den." As for Haligonians, "they walk in their sleep and talk in their sleep and what they say one day they forget the next," while Halifax itself "has got a dose of opium that will send it snoring out of the world, like a feller who falls asleep on the ice on a winter's night."

It is possible that Sam's views of the colony were a little biased. When he was a small boy in Connecticut his mother would frighten him into obedience—making his hair stand up "like a cat's back when she's wrathy"—with the terrible threat: "Sam, if you don't give over acting like Old Scratch, I'll send you off to Nova Scotia, as sure as you are born...."

achieved a form of representative government, but power had remained firmly in the hands of the Governor and his Council—a situation very much like that in the United States before the Revolution—the Governor stating that so important a military station as Halifax and Nova Scotia "must necessarily be governed in accordance with the needs of the Empire," rather, that is to say, than that of its citizens. The Council, known as "The Twelve," held all the reins of power, controlling the colony's finances, appointing its magistrates, and simply vetoing any legislation that threatened their interests.

Joseph Howe, Halifax born and bred, set his sights on the destruction of this oppressive system. In 1835, when he defended himself in a libel suit brought against him by the magistrates, he won a sensational victory for freedom of speech. Finally, after years of further struggle, he was able to oust The Twelve and formed a cabinet of his own party. By this achievement he won for Nova Scotia in 1848 the first Responsible Government—government responsible to the people—granted to any British colony. The great politician went on to play a vigorous part in many of the major issues of the day and was a powerful force in inspiring Nova Scotians to their later achievements.

In 1837 King William died, and Haligonians learned that they were now subjects of the eighteen-year-old Victoria, daughter of the Duke of Kent. This news, "of a new ruler of the foremost Nation of the World," as Howe's *Novascotian* put it, arrived by way of Newfoundland, "word having been brought from Cork by the army transport *Stakesby,* and then relayed by the schooner *Eight Sons.*"

On Coronation Day, the townspeople made a grand time of it. At dawn, the crash of guns "caused Coronation visions to break their morning slumbers," and from then on it was a riot of colour and sound. Ships dressed with flags in the harbour fired off cannon (including HMS *Madagascar,* commanded by Captain Provo Wallis), church bells rang, and the military paraded and loosed off their guns and muskets. Citadel Hill was covered with "mostly ladies, whose gay dresses made the old hill look like a vast tulip bed"; beef, bread, and porter were freely available, and the menfolk climbed greasy poles for silver coins or grappled with greasy pigs let loose among them. The day ended with fireworks "made by artillerymen in the Point Pleasant laboratory" and a champagne-sodden ball for the select few at Government House.

The Micmac were there that day and again in 1840 when the

young queen married Prince Albert—they took part in the cele-bratory procession through the town and were honoured guests at a feast on the Grand Parade where there was "an abundance of fish, fish pies, bread, butter, cheese, cake and porter." Yet in the same year their chiefs—worried by the sinking fortunes of their people—presented a heart-rending petition to the Governor: "Before the white people came, we had plenty of wild roots, plenty of fish and plenty of corn. The skins of Moose and Cariboo were warm to our bodies, we had plenty of good land, we worshipped Kesoult the Great Spirit, we were free and we were happy ... [now] our nation is like a withering leaf in a summer sun." The chiefs signed the document with their tokens—a pipe, the sun, an arrow, a canoe, and the moon.

The new culture, though, was pushing ahead and it was dur-ing the early years of Victoria's long reign that Nova Scotian ship-building came into its own. After having been almost wiped out by privateering during the long war years—it made no sense for Nova Scotians to buy locally made ships when they could be obtained much more cheaply from the French and the Americans—in the next decades it was to become one of the world's most successful industries.

Nova Scotia shipping thrived in support of the Crimean War, which began in 1854. As usual, in times of the Empire's wars, Halifax—incorporated in 1841—was more personally involved. At the outbreak of the war one of the garrison regiments—the 72nd Highlanders—left from the Grand Parade for the battlefields. Later, news arrived of the deaths in action of two townsmen, offi-cers in British regiments; a suitable memorial was erected for them in the Old Burying Ground. During the Indian Mutiny of 1857, another Haligonian—Sir John Inglis—was in command of the heroic defence during the Siege of Lucknow, and a fellow Nova Scotian of African heritage, William Hall, was awarded the colony's first Victoria Cross for gallantry, fighting to relieve him.

But it was after the outbreak of the American Civil War in 1861 that local shipbuilders and shipping merchants surged to a prosperity of which they had only dreamed, and as wealth poured into the city, elegant mansions and public buildings sprung up all over the peninsula. Townspeople were thrilled by a sense of direct involvement when the Confederate raider *Tallahassee* took refuge in the harbour from Union warships and then slipped their blockade down the shallow Eastern Passage—

steered to safety by a local pilot. The war's darker side came home, too, as thousands of young Nova Scotians—including Joseph Howe's son—went off to fight on one side or the other, many never to return.

Ever vigilant, Britannia added to the general prosperity by spending large sums to upgrade the forts and by sending to Halifax a naval squadron and additional regiments, including the illustrious Grenadier Guards. The gilded social scene went into high gear: a whirl of parties and balls, of picnics at Point Pleasant or on the Arm, and of matches made between the daughters of Haligonian merchants or shipping magnates and the aristocratic officers of Her Majesty's armed forces.

As the wars ended, the booming city slumped. This time it was worse than usual. Not only did war business depart, but the development of ironclad steamships wiped out the local ship-building industry—without a nearby source of iron, competition was impossible. The Bluenose century of "wooden ships and iron men" was over. But striding to the forefront of the new age of steamships came the Haligonian Samuel Cunard, who pioneered the transatlantic steamship service; ships bearing his name are still famous for their style and efficiency over one and a half centuries later.

In 1867, during this generally gloomy period, the confedera-tion of Britain's North American colonies was born. Britain was anxious to shed the costs of imperial defence, while the colonies were wary of the intentions of the victorious Union armies to the south (there was much talk there of annexation of the British colonies). Confederation seemed an idea whose time had come. But, deeply loyal to Britain and still confident of their trading prowess, Nova Scotians strongly opposed it and demanded repeal—Joseph Howe even talked of taking up arms against Confederation—but without success. Some of their fears of the new Dominion of Canada were realized as the massive wealth built up during the boom days of shipbuilding began to flow to central Canada, while only goods seemed to flow the other way. Emotions cooled, and as the end of the century drew near, things settled down. There was still the garrison to supply, and Her Majesty's Government was again spending sizeable amounts on the fortress.

In the summer of 1889, Haligonians held a mammoth carnival and quite cheered themselves up. A week of reviews, concerts, and theatrical performances attracted visitors from far and wide, (although American guests seemed more interested in the British warships in the harbour and the quaint social customs, such as tea and muffins at five o' clock). As always, the military provided some of the highlights, including a sham battle in which steamboats and launches attacking the town from behind Georges Island were repelled by the army: "the redcoats' fusillade of musketry made the whole shore from the Tower Woods (Point Pleasant) to the outskirts of the city into a wall of flame." After dark, thousands took the ferry across the harbour through water ablaze with coloured lights, "deafened by the shrieking sirens of ships." This was strong medicine.

Its loyalty to the Crown undimmed, in 1897 the city celebrated Victoria's Diamond Jubilee in grand style. A year later, Canada issued the famous Christmas stamp with a map of the world largely covered in British scarlet and right at the centre, Halifax.

During this period Rudyard Kipling visited the town and—as if to give an imperial stamp of approval—penned a few lines to the fortress:

"Into the mist my guardian prows put forth,
Behind the mist my virgin ramparts lie;
The Warden of the Honour of the North,
Sleepless and veiled am I."

But there were signs that all was not well with the Empire, and by the next Christmas a major blow had been delivered to imperial pride when Boer farmers in South Africa handed the British Army a series of calamitous defeats. Military-minded as ever, Nova Scotians flocked to join the colours; many lost their lives at Paardeberg. The war ended with an imperial victory, but it was clear to the world and to a chastened Britain that, as Kipling wrote, she had been given "no end of a lesson": The Empire's power in the world was limited.

Emboldened by these events, Germany's Kaiser Wilhelm set out to build battle fleets powerful enough to challenge the Royal Navy. British alarm grew, the mother country called her ships home from across the Empire to face the threat, and the naval squadron sailed from the old Halifax dockyard.

With the navy gone there was no need for the garrison. In 1906, the imperial troops marched from the Citadel to the

HALIFAX AND THE RUSSIAN REVOLUTION

*I*n the grey spring of 1917, in the depths of the First World War, the Norwegian-American liner *Kristianifjord* arrived from New York and made her way into the Bedford Basin. On board were eight Bolsheviks whom the naval police had orders to arrest. Among them was Leon Trotsky, later to take on the dictator Stalin in a fight to the death for supreme control of the Soviet Union.

Trotsky and his companions, exiled in America, had heard the news of the Tsar's abdication and were hastening to Russia to join their revolutionary comrades in their seizure of power. The British, knowing that the Bolsheviks planned to take their Russian ally out of the war against Germany, were determined to stop them.

The Bolsheviks were removed from the ship, interrogated in Halifax, and then sent by train to a detention camp in Amherst, Nova Scotia. (Trotsky's wife, also a fiery revolutionary, along with their children were sent under surveillance to a private home in Halifax.) The camp soon rang to the sound of Trotsky's voice, as he tried to convert its German prisoners-of-war to his revolutionary gospel.

International pressure mounted rapidly and within three weeks the Bolsheviks were released—furious over their detention and vowing bitter vengeance on the British and Canadians. They were brought back to Halifax and put on a ship bound for Europe.

The group arrived in Petrogad in time to take part in the October Revolution. As Lenin's right-hand man, Trotsky played a vital role. He then became the driving force behind the Bolshevik army in the bloody civil war that followed and—after the Bolshevik victory—was made foreign minister of the new Soviet state. In a ruthless struggle for supreme power of the Soviet Union, he was defeated by Stalin, who, in 1940, had him murdered.

It is tempting to wonder whether the Russians and Trotsky himself would have been spared some of their calamities if the man had been held longer in Nova Scotia.

transports, and for the first time in 150 years, the city was without its fleet and garrison. There was no question that a certain glory had gone with them.

Modern Times

As Britain, facing the threat from imperial Germany, left its far-flung outposts to fend for themselves, a shadow fell across the Empire. In 1912, when the proud *Titanic* sank with heavy loss of life in the North Atlantic, many thought it signalled the end of British supremacy. The disaster was deeply felt in Halifax: many victims were landed at the port and found a final resting place in the city's burial grounds.

Yet Halifax was stirring, as if from a long sleep, and the new century was to bring the biggest change to the peninsula since 1749.

First, prosperity began to return from new trade in fish, fruit, and Cape Breton steel. Then in 1913 the government in Ottawa decided to pump in millions of dollars to build new harbour and railway facilities—including the cutting of a major railway embankment to the South End—and to generally upgrade the harbour to its rightful status as a seaport of international importance.

As the work got under way, the long peace was coming to an end. While the war clouds gathered in Europe and the need for men, munitions, and supplies became clear, the grey ships of the Royal Navy returned to their old base at the dockyard, and the streets once again streamed with bluejackets. The shore batteries were manned, antisubmarine nets and minefields were laid across the harbour, and the fortress took up its vigilant stance as if nothing had changed.

But now it was a world war and everything was on a much larger—and grimmer—scale. Many thousands of Canadian servicemen left from Halifax for the Western Front. And, as the German U-boats began to maul British shipping, convoys of merchant vessels and transports assembled in Bedford Basin to be escorted across the Atlantic by British warships.

Wartime business boomed again as millions of tons of supplies poured through the port. As in the past, with the influx of thousands of workers and servicemen, morals plummeted. In an attempt to control the situation, in 1916 the authorities imposed a total ban on liquor sales. Overnight, illegal drinking dens—"blind pigs"—sprang up.

On December 6, 1917, a date forever etched on the city's

memory, the long involvement with imperial warfaring had a cataclysmic outcome. An ammunition ship exploded in the harbour, destroying the North End and killing as many as two thousand people, with many more injured and maimed. The United States and the Empire rushed supplies to the stricken city and the work of rebuilding began almost immediately; but it was many years before the devastating effects were left behind. Many noticed the fearful irony: the city which had lain secure behind its fortress against all enemies had been smashed by one mighty blow from within.

In 1919 the troops came home to a shattered city. But the port itself had boomed with the wartime shipping, and the city's shipbuilding industry began to find its feet again. Before long the harbour development that had been interrupted by the war gathered momentum; the work was completed in the late 1920s, leaving Halifax with one of the world's finest port facilities.

The interwar years were drab, a period of modest progress scarred by the Depression. It culminated in 1939 with the visit of King George VI and Queen Elizabeth, an event that Canadians came to view as the "golden interlude." It was a poignant occasion: the old Empire was in obvious decline, and within a few months the mother country herself was to be engaged in a fierce struggle for survival.

With the onset of the Second World War, Halifax fell easily into its familiar role. Once more convoys assembled in the Bedford Basin for their hazardous voyages across the Atlantic while many thousands of Canadian soldiers joined their troopships in the port. Again the fortress became an essential naval and military base. Many of the old defence works were obsolete, and aircraft based at Shearwater Air Station were now Halifax's primary defence while, to beat off attacks by enemy aircraft, the harbour was ringed by anti-aircraft guns centred in the old Citadel.

In this war the struggle to keep open the lifeline from Halifax to Britain—herself under attack and in 1940 threatened by invasion—was a more desperate one. An indication of this was the swift demolition of the old eighteenth- and nineteenth-century dockyard buildings and their replacement by modern structures. The new facilities were needed not just for the Royal Navy but for the hugely expanded Royal Canadian Navy whose ships were to play a valorous part in the deadly Battle of the Atlantic.

Halifax was badly overburdened. The population had

expanded by close to 50 per cent as war workers flocked in, while the sailors of many nations thronged the streets. As before, the quality of life and of morals gradually deteriorated. When victory was announced in May 1945, the authorities decided to close all liquor stores to forestall trouble. Frustration with wartime conditions boiled over and sailors began a major riot in the downtown area, setting fire to trams, smashing their way into liquor stores, and looting shops.

In this war there were some dark echoes of the 1917 catastrophe. In 1942, the navy had had to sink by gunfire an American ammunition ship that had caught fire in the harbour off Georges Island. Then, two months after the VE Day Riots, the large magazine in Bedford Basin—crammed to overflowing with ammunition brought back from the war—exploded. Although residents of the North End were evacuated, little damage was done to the city—the magazine had been designed to contain just such a blast.

Once again, troops returned to a jarred city. Nova Scotian regiments received a tumultuous welcome in the streets, while ships' whistles, factory sirens, church bells, and people joined in joyful cacophony. It was a raw counterpoint to the casualty lists; the city and the province had paid again a heavy price in its native sons.

With peace, Halifax resumed its gentle progress. St. Mary's University built a new campus in the South End, while towards the centre of the city many of the old sites that had in some cases been occupied for almost two centuries by military headquarters, barracks, and hospitals were taken over by the city. Some real planning could begin.

In the 1960s Halifax began a major renovation, sweeping away several derelict areas. Although most of it was welcome and long overdue, the demolition of Africville, a black shanty town overlooking Bedford Basin, was much lamented by its inhabitants. It was clear to all that a rich community spirit had been diminished.

This major change to the city's face (only the port development of the 1920s came close to it) rushed ahead more or less unchecked, and it was only a spirited battle by concerned citizens that saved from oblivion the Historic Properties area and the time-honoured views from Citadel Hill. As it was, several buildings of genuine historic worth were bulldozed to make way for faceless high-rises.

Along with the urban development, the Canadian navy began to expand and modernize its shore establishments, and Canadian vessels would often be joined at the dockyard by NATO vessels. Perhaps more important for the city, the strong peacetime military and naval presence meant that the old grinding economic cycle of boom in war and bust in peace had been broken.

The British Empire that gave Halifax birth is long gone. Created, as a British statesman put it, "in a fit of absence of mind," it was an empire of "muddled grandeur," and along with the vision and the romance there was also greed and sometimes brutality. It was, though, the largest empire in history, and its effects, perhaps most notably in the spreading of the vigorous English language across the planet, were far-reaching. And, its outline foreseen by Joseph Howe, the Commonwealth—the Empire's heir—endures as a world forum for the ex-colonies.

Halifax, for so long embroiled in imperial campaigns, figuring so large in the Empire's misfortunes and so little in its affluence, is today a peaceable centre of commerce and learning. Its streets wreathed in memories, the city rests contentedly on its peninsula, surveying the vivid spectacle of its past and the promise of its future.

Around the harbour, the old forts lie crumbling, their military role long overtaken by ever-newer technologies. Yet the harbour and the naval dockyard continue as they have for almost two and a half centuries: Halifax holds to its role as a valuable seaport and as a bastion in the continent's defence.

The Fortress

This section describes the growth of the fortress and indicates the tour on which the various defence works can be explored. For example, **Cambridge Battery (3)** *indicates that the battery is described in Tour 3—Point Pleasant Park.*

Halifax—the city, its naval dockyard, and the fortress shielding them from attack—was a powerful imperial bastion. In the eighteenth century it was the base for the conquest of Canada. In the next century it became the new colony's guardian against the expanding republic to the south. Then, in its most urgent role, in this century's world wars Halifax was the gateway for the flow of men, weapons, and supplies to a desperate and embattled mother country, and—in the second war—the chief British command centre and base for the Battle of the Atlantic.

Such a distinguished role did not come without great effort

and ingenuity. Much of this went into building the many different works of the fortress, usually urged on by some new threat to the Empire. In all, forts and batteries were to be built at over forty sites in and around Halifax, and many of these—for example, Citadel Hill and Georges Island—were to have several more modern forts built over the ruins of the previous ones.

Halifax Harbour at the Height of Empire (Sandham, 1878).

The defences at first clustered tightly around the town to fend off Indian attacks from the forest. Then, as the fortress grew and technology advanced, they gradually spread across the peninsula, to the islands and to the forbidding bluffs guarding the harbour entrance until, at the height of Empire, the fortress was impregnable. No enemy was ever to make an attempt on it, and across two centuries the mighty fortress's guns never fired a shot in anger.

"A Position Of Extraordinary Natural Strength ..."
Its strategic position astride the sea routes of the Atlantic combined with the superb qualities of its harbour gave Halifax an enormous role in imperial expansion and defence.

The strategic value was obvious. Jutting out into the Atlantic close to both the St. Lawrence River with its access to Canada, and to the eastern seaboard of the United States, Halifax was a wonderfully located base from which the Royal Navy could exercise British power. Whether the adversary was the French in Quebec, the mutinous Americans to the south, or German U-boats prowling the Atlantic, Halifax again and again demonstrated its worth as an imperial base.

The harbour itself had "extraordinary natural strength" as one imperial planner put it. First there was the immense deep-water anchorage of Bedford Basin, sheltered alike from Atlantic storms and enemy attack. Then there was the relative ease of defending the narrow harbour mouth by means of forts placed on the high bluffs, on McNabs Island, or on the peninsula itself. In all, the harbour and its entrance resembled nothing so much as an enormous upturned rum bottle whose mouth could be easily stoppered. In 1861 the Duke of Newcastle described it as, "In all probability the finest harbour in the world."

For much of the city's history a naval attack on Halifax stood little chance of success against the harbour defences and the all-powerful Royal Navy. The real threat was felt to come from an overland attack. This concern, held well into the twentieth century, was eased by the knowledge that defences could be placed across the narrow neck connecting the peninsula to the mainland—a useful terra firma equivalent of 'stoppering the bottle.'

These natural strengths combined with a healthy climate (Yellow Fever at the navy's base at Bermuda, by contrast, was a major problem) and an intensely loyal population (only during the American Revolution and just after Confederation was there any question of this), to complete Halifax's superb qualities as sentinel of the North Atlantic.

The Early Years

In 1749 Governor Cornwallis pushed the new settlers to build up the defences against Micmac raiding parties. Completed over the next few years, these defences consisted of a half-circle of five small forts linked together by a log palisade. The central fort in the ring, close to the summit of the commanding hill, was named the **Citadel (2)**.

To protect the harbour, in 1750 a strong battery—an emplacement for cannon—was placed on **Georges Island (7)**, which was located conveniently in the harbour, like an anchored man o'war. Another battery was built at the **Eastern Passage (3)**, on the

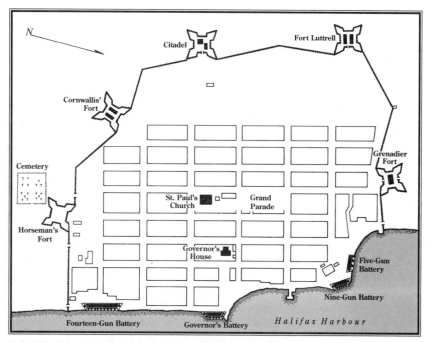

Early Halifax defences: Five wooden forts linked by palisades protected the town against attacks from the landward side; four sea batteries defended the town's harbour side.

Dartmouth side of the harbour. These two batteries worked together to prevent enemy vessels from approaching the town and the naval dockyard.

A few years later three batteries were built on the town's waterfront to protect it against attacks from the sea. In 1761, when the three works had deteriorated, a small battery was erected opposite Georges Island to replace them; gradually expanded and more and more heavily armed, the new work became known as **Grand Battery (7)**. For over a hundred years this—together with the Georges Island and Eastern Passage batteries—constituted the main line of the harbour defences.

The harbour was, however, far from secure. The short ranges of smooth-bore cannon meant there were worryingly large patches of water that were not covered by the forts (see smooth-bore cannon ranges map, page 32). In fact, it was over a century before Halifax's guns could really defend the harbour. In the meantime, the Royal Navy had to do the lion's share in protecting its base, to the extent of sometimes mooring warships in the sea channels.

Nevertheless, Halifax was relatively safe from seaward attack. Yet the defenders soon saw that they were still vulnerable to overland attacks. So a string of three **blockhouses (5)** was built from the Northwest Arm to Bedford Basin (the first close to the current Armdale Rotary, and the last about where the entrance to Fairview Cemetery is now).

After the fall of Louisbourg in 1758 many of the defences were allowed to go to ruin, but in 1762 a French attack on Newfoundland startled the town and its defenders out of their growing sense of security. Fearing an attack on the town, they quickly threw up new batteries on Point Pleasant designed to harass enemy ships trying to enter the harbour or the Northwest Arm (from where enemy troops could march on the town). Two of these defences, later much enlarged and modified, became known as the **Point Pleasant Battery (3)** and the **Northwest Arm Battery (3)**. In addition, a chain and timber boom was stretched from Point Pleasant to the opposite shore, providing a physical obstacle to ships attempting to sail up the Arm; it was covered by an armed sloop moored inside the boom.

The American Revolution sparked a new flurry of defensive activity. The rebellious Americans had no navy and the main concern was that they would attack by land. Existing forts were repaired and new ones built: **Fort Needham (5)** to the north of the town to defend the critically important dockyard, and **Fort Massey (6)** to the south to support the main fort on Citadel Hill in its landward defence. In addition, the dockyard was further protected from land attack by a string of blockhouses and bastions (5)—in fact, it was far better protected than the town.

When France entered the war, concern shifted back to the harbour defences, so a new and distinctly eccentric fort was built on Citadel Hill (the second Citadel—see plan on page 29). In 1793, just before the arrival of Prince Edward, the General Officer Commanding gave his name to the new small work he put up at Point Pleasant—**Fort Ogilvie (3)**, built on high ground and designed to support the two batteries (Point Pleasant and Northwest Arm) already located on the shoreline. The fort was the last one to be given a name other than that of a member of the Royal family for some years.

The Second Citadel (1784).

A Royal Fortress

Prince Edward, the Duke of Kent, has been described as "a Prince who loved to build forts." Perceiving a threat to British interests in the Western Hemisphere—specifically Halifax—from Revolutionary France, with a breezy efficiency he set about throwing up new works and repairing old ones.

One of his most important projects was the complete rebuilding of the Citadel to a simpler and far better plan (the third Citadel). But the innovation of which he was most proud was his "telegraph" system. This used a combination of flags and balls raised on signal masts for communication between the elements of his command—including his love nest on Bedford Basin. The system ran south from the Citadel and Point Pleasant to Sambro Island, and across Nova Scotia to Annapolis Royal.

Prince Edward also developed a passion for heavily armed and strongly built Martello towers, which he erected at the main defence points—the first of many to be dotted around the Empire. The first was built on the highest site above Point Pleasant and was intended as a central fortification covering the other batteries on the point; one of these was a small defence work named **Chain Battery (3),** designed to cover the chain boom that was again stretched across the Northwest Arm from Point Pleasant. Edward followed the tower on the Point with ones on the Eastern Passage and at a new site on the high bluffs southwest of Point Pleasant. Two further towers were to be built after his departure

POWDERED HAIR: THE DUKE'S ORDERS

*E*dward, Duke of Kent, was trained in the Prussian military tradition. From Halifax on July 1, 1800, he issued General Orders for British officers serving in North America, laying down the approved hair and queue (what we might call pigtail) style with a fierce attention to detail that leaves one breathless—and thankful that times have changed.

"The hair of all officers is to be cut according to the following form. Brush top as close as possible admitting the Comb to lay between the scissors and the head, the hair of the top being gradually left a little longer as it approaches the ear so as to admit of being at all times turned at the sides with a curling iron but the ear to be perfectly bare and at all times free from any powder, no side locks whatever being allowed of, the hind hair to be parted off from the top in the shape of an Horse shoe from a straight line taken one inch behind the ear, and on no account to be thinned from the Horse shoe but to be left to grow in one equal level length down. Queues are invariably to be worn tied at the distance of two inches from the Head showing seven of Ribbon and two of hair at the bottom with a bow tied close to the top and the ends of the bow as well as those of the ribbon falling down five inches—Grenadier, Fusilier and Light Infantry Officers, when wearing their Caps are then to appear with their hair plaited, and a ribbon ornament or trollop flush fixed close to the hair under the plait. The plait to be tied close to the head, the hair to be turned up at the length of two inches from the tye, braided as flat as possible to appear without stiffness and to be fixed up with a Comb the plait covering the whole of the Comb, which should be about one and an half inch wide at the utmost, the bottom of the plait being half an inch wider than the top and at all times the hair is to be well filled with Powder and Pomatum."

for England, on Georges Island and Mauger Beach.

In a final flourish, Edward graced his new forts with the names of his family. He named the new work on Citadel Hill **Fort George (2),** after his father, the King (the street and the island had, after all, been named after the previous monarch); the Martello tower at Point Pleasant he named the **Prince of Wales Tower (3),** after the future George IV; the fort on the bluffs, **York Redoubt (4),** after his brother the Duke of York; a new fort on Georges Island, **Fort Charlotte (7),** after the Queen; and he named the tower on the Eastern Passage **Fort Clarence (3),** after the future William IV.

Of these works, only the Prince of Wales Tower and a section of the tower at York Redoubt remain. And the Old Town Clock, which Edward had intended as the Garrison Clock, continues to chime the hours away on the side of Citadel Hill.

Sentinel of the Sea

With Napoleon's final defeat at the Battle of Waterloo in 1815, Great Britain's supremacy was unchallenged. This dominance was exercised largely through her powerful "instrument of universal order," the Royal Navy, cruising from good, well-protected bases scattered across the world. The peace that now descended was a peace of the sea.

Halifax was a key base, but only a few years after Waterloo most of the fortifications were in ruins. Except for the Martello Towers, they had been built of wood, sod, and earth, and the Nova Scotian climate had little difficulty in breaking them down—sometimes in the space of a few seasons.

In 1825 the Duke of Wellington, amid fears of a new outbreak of hostilities with the United States, sent out a commission to Halifax to investigate the situation. Of the fortress, there was little to show at Halifax for seventy-five years of effort and expense. The commission, realizing the wastefulness of spending vast amounts in wartime only to neglect the works in times of peace, recommended that the funds be spent to make the fortress permanent.

Designed as the central and impregnable strongpoint of the entire fortress, the construction of the present Citadel (the fourth one) began. Gradually many of the other works were rebuilt using masonry, brick, and later, concrete. The original positions of these forts having been, for the most part, well chosen, the

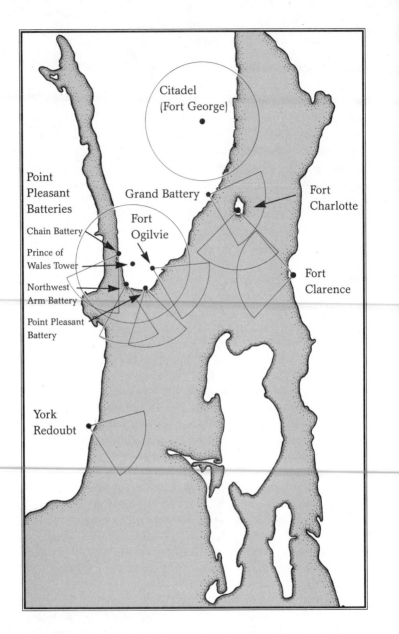

The fortress in the early 1880s showing the range of smooth-bore cannon. The main defence line centred on Fort Charlotte, on Georges Island.

new structures simply went on top of the old.

But hardly had the Royal Engineers completed the reconstruction of the forts than most of their efforts were rendered useless by stunning advances in technology.

For centuries, weapons of war had changed little. Smooth-bore cannon fired round projectiles; the only significant development was that of the size and weight of the cannon ball. Then in the 1850s the rifled gun was introduced, using grooves cut in a spiral pattern along the length of the inner surface of the barrel to give a rapid rotation to the projectile, which was now also more aerodynamic (the familiar "bullet" shape). This shell had far greater velocity, accuracy, and destructive power. Also about this time, the first ironclad ships appeared; by contrast with wooden-hulled ships they seemed almost indestructible.

These inventions shocked engineers who became quickly aware that their forts—lovingly evolved from theories handed down for centuries—would not long survive a battering from rifled guns mounted in armoured ships. (Although it was not to be admitted until the 1880s, one of the first theoretical casualties of this was the new Citadel whose ramparts—massive as they were—could clearly not withstand the new guns.) A radical reconstruction of the fortress was begun. It was also clear that enemy vessels with their far-ranging and highly destructive weapons had to be stopped much further out from the harbour than before. So in the 1860s—the modifications accelerated by fear of British involvement in the American Civil War—the main defence line shifted from the old line centred on Georges Island to one between Point Pleasant Park and McNabs Island; two new works, **Cambridge Battery (3)** and **Ives Point Battery (7)**, were constructed, and the entire fortress was rearmed with the new rifled weapons. At last, the stopper at the harbour mouth could be used to firmly seal off Halifax from the open sea.

After the expensive modifications were completed at the end of the 1860s, the old superiority of forts over ships reasserted itself. With its new armament of 70 heavy guns and with a total of over 360 guns either mounted or in storage, the Halifax fortress had become invincible.

Empire's Zenith
Nowhere outside the home country was the Union Jack so firmly planted as at Halifax and—after Great Britain herself—the

fortress was the first in the Empire to be armed with rifled weapons. It was by then pre-eminent in the famous quadrilateral of Royal Navy bases—Halifax, Gibraltar, Malta, and Bermuda.

There was, then, no question of giving up Halifax, when in 1871, Her Majesty's Government decided to withdraw British regular troops from the Canadian interior. The dockyard, well protected by the fortress, was simply far too valuable a base for the Royal Navy, and letting go of Halifax would mean abandoning imperial interests in the entire Western Hemisphere.

So as the Empire moved to its brash and glittering climax, the work on the forts went on. Accelerating technology led to still newer and more powerful weapons in the fortress's armoury. The early rifled muzzle-loaders were replaced by guns that could be loaded from the breech, while quick-firing guns (to stop the new high-speed torpedo boats), searchlights, high explosives, and mines all found their place in the evolving defence complex. As weapons evolved, so did the need to stop an enemy as far away from the town and dockyard as possible. In the 1880s and '90s the engineers built new and stronger forts closer to the harbour mouth, making this outer line the strongest of the harbour defences. **Fort McNab (7)**, mounting the heaviest gun in the fortress, and **Fort Hugonin (7)** were constructed on McNabs Island; **Sandwich Battery (4)**, the last fort to be constructed by the British at Halifax, was built seaward of York Redoubt.

Of course, cruising far at sea from its powerful Nova Scotian base was the Royal Navy. It had never seemed more magnificent: its ships were modern, and there were almost four times as many of them as had its nearest competitor. Around it there hung "legends and victorious memories, mellowed by age, gunsmoke, rum and saltspray" of the great Nelsonian tradition. This splendid force was a crucial argument against attacking Halifax.

So by 1897—the year of Victoria's Diamond Jubilee, when the Queen-Empress ruled over a quarter of the world's surface—the fortress was formidable indeed. An enemy vessel attempting to gain entry to the harbour would have to pass three daunting lines of defence. At the harbour entrance was the *first line* of new and powerful forts, with guns that could range miles out to sea. Should any vessels elude the outer forts they would be faced by the *second line,* which brought a tremendous concentration of fire to bear on the sea between McNabs Island and Point Pleasant, backed by a minefield in the same area. The *third line* was in the

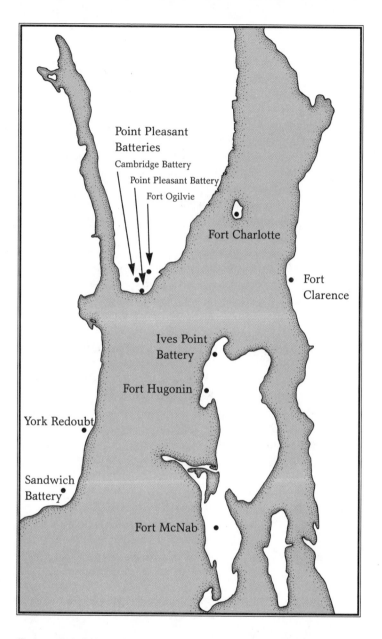

Point Pleasant
Batteries

Cambridge Battery

Point Pleasant Battery

Fort Ogilvie

Fort Charlotte

Fort
Clarence

Ives Point
Battery

Fort Hugonin

York Redoubt

Sandwich
Battery

Fort McNab

The fortress in the final years of Queen Victoria's reign. (Gun Ranges are not shown—Halifax's guns reached many miles out to sea.) The main defence line was now Fort McNab/Sandwich Battery.

VICTORIA'S DIAMOND JUBILEE

On June 22, 1897, in a massive international festival, the largest—and, many felt, the greatest—Empire in history celebrated sixty years of the Queen-Empress Victoria's reign. In London, the capital of the Empire, it was a sight perhaps never equalled as hundreds of princes and ambassadors and tens of thousands of troops rode in a glittering display of imperial strength and splendour. In the middle rode the old Queen in her sombre black, weeping intermittently from sheer joy.

The world applauded. A French newspaper declared that Rome had been equalled if not surpassed, while the *New York Times* generously owned the United States part of "the Greater Britain which seems so plainly destined to dominate the planet." Sternly conscious of the port's role in imperial defence, the Halifax Herald under the heading "THE ADMISSION OF AN ENEMY" reported the *New York Sun*'s description of the Jubilee procession as, "The Most Marvellous Sight the Sun Ever Looked Down Upon." (Perhaps the *Herald* was making up for its giddiness in an earlier report headed, "The Mystic Mysticism of the British Throne and the World's Greatest Queen").

In Halifax Harbour, at six in the morning, warships fired 21-gun salutes as HMS *Crescent* imperiously displayed the Royal Standard at the mainmast, and throughout the day Halifax thundered and rang amid the most spectacular celebrations in its history. The gunfire from the Royal Navy squadron was augmented at the noon salute by sailors and marines firing their rifles in unison after every tenth gun. Shots echoed from the Citadel and the surrounding forts and from repeated 60-gun salutes fired by massed artillery on the Common. Church bells chimed across the city.

The day included a regatta and various excursions in the harbour, six British and Canadian regiments laid on a military display, and in the evening, the citizens of Dartmouth lit huge bonfires on their side of the water. Thousands thrilled to a torchlight tattoo by the regimental bands on the

Common. At the climax, the soldiers lit hundreds of Chinese lanterns and then marched and countermarched under the bobbing lights. The bands played the final "God Save the Queen," a picture of Her Majesty's face was illuminated, and a spontaneous roar from the crowd "left no doubt of Halifax's loyalty." As the grand finale, a "bouquet of sixty rockets" from the *Crescent* blossomed over the harbour.

After their tumultuous outpouring of loyalty, Haligonians retired to bed with hoarse throats and ringing ears, but, along with many millions of others, happy in the security and glory of a great Empire. It was a moment rich in significance. Only two years later the imperial spirit was severely shaken by a string of defeats in the South African War; within twenty years it was broken in the horror of the trenches on the Western Front.

....

AN IMPORTANT CAUTION:

Ladies who are accustomed to wear their dresses extremely low in the back and bosom, or off shoulders, are particularly requested to beware of a person who has for some time past frequented all places of public amusement, and many private parties. He is an elderly gentleman of venerable appearance and correct manner; his constant practice, when he observes a lady clad in the manner above described, is: with an almost imperceptible and apparently accidental pressure of a little instrument which he carries in his hand, to imprint the following words upon her back or shoulders—NAKED BUT NOT ASHAMED. The stain is like that produced by lunar-caustic; washing will not remove it and it becomes more visible by exposure to the air, so that nothing but a covering can conceal it. It is said that several ladies were marked last summer at various places of fashionable resort, and that they cannot, even now, strip for company without displaying this indelible badge of disgrace.

From the Acadian Recorder, *September 28, 1816, Halifax.*

harbour itself, the old line made up of the batteries on Georges Island and Fort Clarence, supported by the Citadel.

As one historian said, not even the Royal Navy could run past such defences.

The Twentieth Century

In 1906 Britain, fearful of the German Kaiser's growing threat to the home islands, withdrew the garrison and the Royal Navy squadron from Halifax. Within a few years, however, the British were back. Halifax was to play its most vital role during the two world wars: as the fortified harbour from which fighting men and war supplies departed for Europe and also as a key military base. The old forts faded in importance as newer technology, particularly aircraft, made their stone ramparts and fixed positions obsolete. But they still had a meaningful part to play.

In World War I, the *first line* of defence remained the forts at the Battery, a new fort completed in 1917 by the Canadian military on a hill north of York Redoubt. Reflecting the new and deadly threat from the German U-boats, the *second line* was an antisubmarine net between Point Pleasant and McNabs Island, covered by guns at the Point Pleasant, Ives Point, and Hugonin Batteries. The *third line* of defence consisted of an antisubmarine net strung east and west across the harbour from Georges Island, protected by quick-firing guns at Fort Charlotte. Late in the war, a seaplane base was constructed on the Eastern Passage for the use of American naval aircraft.

As World War II brought air power fully into play, aircraft flying from **Shearwater Air Station** (3) became Halifax's first line of defence. This active defence was backed by the harbour defences, all of which were then seaward of York Redoubt, which became the Fire Command centre. An antisubmarine net strung between Mauger Beach on McNabs Island and the cove below York Redoubt was covered by the new **York Shore** (4) and **Strawberry** (7) **Batteries.** The old second and third lines of defence were completely eclipsed. Only Fort Ogilvie had a role—as a training battery.

In modern times—the age of nuclear submarines, sea-skimming missiles, and supersonic aircraft—Halifax's role continues. The dockyard functions as it has for over two centuries, now serving the graceful vessels of the Canadian Navy, and periodically, NATO fleets, which usually include at least one ship of the

Royal Navy. Aircraft from Shearwater Air Station sometimes thunder overhead, the sound an echo of a day when signal and practice cannon boomed from forts and ships.

The Canadian Parks Service now has custody of the old defence system and has restored the most historically intriguing sites. The others, once part of a mighty fortress designed to withstand the greatest violence that men could hurl against it, are being quietly conquered by the woods and the sea-laden air.

The Old Town

Tour 1 covers the sights of the Old Town, including major points of interest from the eighteenth and nineteenth centuries, and the harbour front. As you wander, be sure to look for the blue Registered Heritage Property markers, which identify buildings of unique heritage value.

If you are pressed for time, you can take the Short Tour. This covers the central area—within the bounds of the former log walls—but omits Government House, the Old Burying Ground, and other points of interest. To take the Short Tour, start at the beginning of Tour 1 and follow the directions for the Short Tour when you come to them.

St. Paul's and the Parade (Short, 1759).

Introduction

Note: Tour 1 begins on facing page.

In the summer of 1749, Halifax was created on a forested hillside at Chebucto harbour. Designed to support and protect the vital Royal Navy base, the town was for several years surrounded by log palisades and blockhouses to fend off French or Indian attacks. These wooden defences are long gone, but there are surviving features from within the wall, notably the Grand Parade and St. Paul's Church—and many more from the later eighteenth and early nineteenth centuries.

Sheltered beneath a succession of forts on Citadel Hill, Halifax was above all a naval and garrison town. For one and a half centuries, richly coloured uniforms were everywhere, and the streets echoed to the thump and blare of martial music and the crash of signal cannon. And, sandwiched as it was between the taverns and bawdy-houses of Barrack (now Brunswick) Street, known as "Knock-'Em-Down Street," and the drinking dens of Water Street, known as "The Beach," the town provided plenty of distractions for off-duty soldiers and sailors.

The town also engendered a healthy civil society. From the earliest days merchants prospered, usually as suppliers to the military, and as the town grew, graceful public buildings appeared. In the early 1800s Government House and Province House were built, soon to become the scene of momentous political events. Later in that century, as the home port of sailors, merchants, and shipbuilders, Halifax became the powerhouse for the province's enormous influence and prosperity during the age of sail.

In this century, Halifax has been a crucial seaport and military base in two world wars. After extensive redevelopment in the 1960s the city has a modern commercial face while continuing to fulfil its old role as a seaport of international significance.

....
START TOUR

Start and end point: Grand Parade, in the centre of town bounded by Duke and Prince, and Barrington and Argyle Streets. (Note: If you prefer to begin the tour at Historic Properties, simply start your tour at the Historic Properties section on page 69, and when you reach the end of the tour, return to the beginning of the tour—at the Grand Parade below.)

Time: One to three hours for basic tour; allow additional time for the Art Gallery of Nova Scotia and the Maritime Museum.

The **Grand Parade** is Halifax's oldest recognizable feature, laid out at the new settlement's heart in 1749 as a drilling and mustering ground for troops. Since then it has seen an unbroken line of ceremonial and civic events. Every morning for a hundred years, a regimental band played here for half an hour, after which the King's troops in their scarlet coats mounted guard—a great

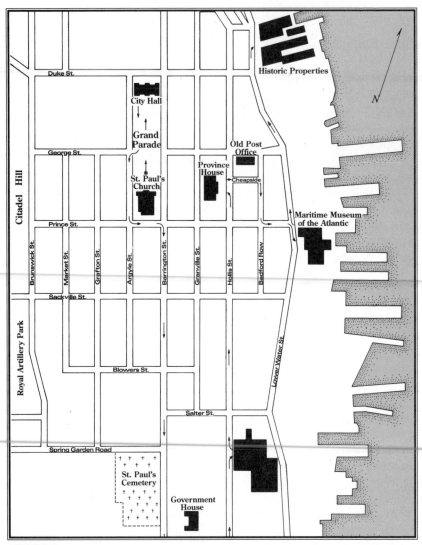

Tour 1

The Old Town

attraction for country visitors. On summer evenings, a young officer reported in 1787, the band would play "when all the belles
and beaux of the place promenade, and the band remains to play
as long as they walk."

The Parade has seen a profusion of equally colourful but less
orderly events. In the first year the townspeople were gathered
here and warned of a coming attack by French and Indians;

though no attack came, the announcement accelerated the building of the town's log palisade defences. Here the town criers read their proclamations. The well-to-do came to the Parade to hire sedan chairs rather than risk the odorous mud. People convicted of criminal acts—including one Sicilian nobleman—were sometimes paraded here before being hauled off to jail. In 1799 huge bonfires were lit on the Parade to welcome back Prince Edward, the Duke of Kent, while in 1863 the results of a greasy pole competition held here so displeased a British regiment that they went on a destructive rampage through the town.

The **cenotaph** is located close to the centre of the Parade. Patterned after the Cenotaph in Whitehall, London, it honours the memory of the fallen in three wars in this century. This movingly simple monument stands in place of an equestrian statue of King George II, which was planned in the eighteenth century but never erected.

At the north end of the Parade is the **City Hall**. Begun in 1887, this Victorian edifice occupies the original site of Dalhousie University, which moved to its current location after twelve years of heated debate. The city has now outgrown the building, and many of its offices are in rented space in the immediate area.

St. Paul's Church
Visitors are welcome throughout the year; during the summer months a guide is in attendance.

At the south end of the Parade is **St. Paul's Church,** the first Anglican cathedral outside the British Isles, the oldest Protestant church in Canada, and the city's oldest building.

It was completed in 1750, one year after Halifax's settlement. Founded by a proclamation of George II, the design was inspired by St. Peter's Church in London, whose architect was a pupil of Sir Christopher Wren (the architect of London's St. Paul's Cathedral). Appropriately enough for the early years, much of its funding came from taxes on rum.

Governor Cornwallis sent his adjutant Richard Bulkeley to Boston for the church's timber, which was shipped to Halifax as a prefabricated frame. The old structure remains sturdily in place although it was remodelled in the nineteenth century from its classical simplicity to a more Victorian taste. The church's three bells, still in use today, were cast in London in 1812.

In addition to serving the townspeople, the church was the

garrison chapel for many years. The Sunday service was colourful. Led by their bands, the various regiments marched in full
dress to the church. When the Governor entered, he was "followed by a brilliant display of gold lace and feathers, the clank of
sabres and spurs, and the shaking of plumed hats." Officers and
ladies sat in the pews, while common soldiers sat out of view in
the galleries—the infantry on one side, the artillery and cavalry
on the other. Lacking in pomp but not in spiritual fervour, in
1769 a special service in their own language was held in the
church for the Micmac.

Entering the church and walking up the main aisle towards
the **Chancel,** there is a sense of spacious dignity and of deep allegiances. In the Chancel are wooden plaques dating from the early
days of the church and the organ, which is the church's fifth. (It
was installed in 1908; the first organ is said to have been taken
from a Spanish ship, captured in 1765.)

To the right of the Chancel, in the **Baptistry,** are two fonts,
the smaller of which dates from the era of Charles I, a century
before the church was built. Mounted on the wall just behind the
font is a wooden offering box dating from the eighteenth century.

To the left of the Chancel is the **Chapel.** In the side wall next
to the communion table is the oldest stained glass window in the
church, dating from 1868. On either side of the window are
memorial tablets to two of the numerous military and naval men
honoured in the church. St. Paul's is reputed to have the greatest
number of memorial tablets of any church in North America.

On the floor just to the left of the Chancel steps, a small **brass
plaque** marks the burial place of Bishop Charles Inglis, the first
Anglican bishop in the overseas British possessions. Twenty other
leading citizens are buried beneath the church floor, including
Richard Bulkeley and the Baron de Seitz who was buried in full
uniform with sabre and spurs; following an old German custom,
an orange was placed in his right hand to signify the end of an
aristocratic line.

Immediately to your left at the head of the main aisle is the
Royal Pew, reserved for the British Monarch or an appointed
representative. George III's coat of arms is affixed to the side of the
pew.

The coats of arms on the face of the gallery represent the
Anglican Church of Canada and various dioceses, while on the
face of the gallery towards the rear of the church is the Royal

Coat of Arms flanked by the arms of Nova Scotia on the right and of the city of Halifax on the left.

Hatchments are hung on the gallery walls. These diamond-shaped panels were commonly used by prominent men in the seventeenth and eighteenth centuries. At his death, the man's hatchment was immediately hung on the front door of his house and then carried in the funeral procession to the church, where it was deposited. Among the hatchments are those of Richard Bulkeley, Governor Parr, the Baron de Seitz, and Phillip Durell, Vice-Admiral of the Blue.

In the west gallery wall—third window from the back of the church—is the noted **"Explosion window,"** shattered by the Great Explosion of 1917. It is said to resemble in silhouette an assistant who served at the church in 1750.

On leaving the church, note another relic of the Explosion: a piece of window frame embedded in the wall above the memorial entrance arch. Also of interest is the gravestone of two seamen killed in the fierce engagement between their ship, HMS *Shannon* and the American frigate *Chesapeake* in 1813.

···· *Turn left towards Argyle Street and the hill as you leave the church.*

To your right at the corner of George Street is the **National School** (1817), the oldest school building in the city. Here boys and girls were taught in separate classes by the town's leading citizens, including the Countess of Dalhousie, the wife of the Governor. In 1902 it became the home of the Victoria School of Art and Design founded by Anna Leonowens, the former governess to the children of the King of Siam (the Anna of *The King and I*).

In front of you across Argyle Street is a Georgian house. Built in 1813, it was once the home of James Boyle Uniacke, the first Premier of Nova Scotia after the granting of Responsible Government.

···· *Turn left along Argyle Street and walk to the corner of Prince Street.*

From the sidewalk there is a good view of the church's "Explosion window" (third from the left, upper level). Across Argyle Street on the corner is a typical pre-Confederation (1863) townhouse with gabled dormers.

Across Prince Street, on the corner is the **Carleton Hotel,** once the elegant residence of Richard Bulkeley, a cavalryman and adjutant to Governor Cornwallis. Built in the late 1700s of stone from the defeated Fortress of Louisbourg (the stone had originally come from Caen in Normandy), it was for a time the meeting place of the navy's Court of Vice-Admiralty. As a justice of the town, Bulkeley once summoned nine Royal Navy captains here and roundly censured them for their unbridled use of press gangs to fill out their crews. Here, too, he entertained General Wolfe, just before his departure for the fateful battle on the Plains of Abraham at Quebec.

···· *Turn left down Prince Street and proceed to the corner of Barrington Street.*

S H O R T   T O U R   To take the abbreviated tour of the Old Town, continue another two blocks down Prince Street to Hollis and turn left. Then turn to page 58. To proceed with the full tour, continue below.

···· *Turn right on Barrington Street.*

Named for Viscount Barrington of Ardglass, from the city's founding **Barrington Street** was Halifax's principal thoroughfare. Lined with intriguing Victorian (and one Georgian) commercial buildings, this section of the street was also the premier shopping district. In the VE Day Riots in 1945 the street took the brunt of thousands of servicemen's—and some townspeople's—frustration with wartime conditions. In the 1950s the major stores moved elsewhere.

The second building from the corner on the near side of the street is the **Forrester Building** (at 1678). Built before 1822, it is the oldest commercial building on Barrington Street and one of the few remaining Georgian shops in the city. Next to it at 1672-74 is **Wright's Building** (built in 1895), where the radio pioneer Marconi once operated an experimental broadcasting station.

As you walk along Barrington, on your right in the middle of the next block you will see a trio of Victorian neogothic buildings that capture the spirit of their age. The spire of **number 1588**

Prince of Wales' triumphal procession on Barrington Street (Andrews, 1860).

points to its original use as the Church of England Institute, head-quarters of the Anglican bishops; in 1907 it opened as the Nickel, the city's first permanent movie house. Next to it, at **1580,** was the City Club, built in 1886 for young men of the monied classes. **Number 1572** originally housed St. Mary's Total Abstinence and Benevolent Society; nine hundred guests attended its opening in 1891, mindfully sipping nonalcoholic beverages and perhaps thinking that Virtue had the champagne-soaked gentlemen next door surrounded.

On the left hand side of the street in the next block, on the corner of Salter Street, is the **Freemason's Hall,** built in 1924. Near this spot in the 1750s was a wooden blockhouse named Horseman's Fort, in which was the south gate of the town. From this point, along the line of Salter Street down to the harbour, ran the log palisade south wall of the town. (You have, then, just walked to the perimeter of the Old Town from its centre, the Grand Parade.)

On your right as you approach the traffic lights at Spring Garden Road is **St. Mary's Basilica** (1820), the spire of which is

FROM CHULALONGKORN'S COURT TO HALIFAX

*D*uring the formidable expansion of the British Empire, Anna Leonowens made her own powerful mark. Today, through the musical *The King and I*, she is a well-known figure of the age.

Her formative years seemed altogether imperial. She let it be known that she was born in Wales in 1834 to a British Army officer father and educated at a private school. In India, at the age of seventeen, she married an army major. Only seven years later, her husband died of sunstroke in Singapore after a tiger hunt—having ridden through the heat of the day to be with her. His officer companions set the tiger's claws into a brooch that she wore daily for the rest of her life.

This romantic view of her early years seems to have been an enhanced one, created partly by the redoubtable Anna—to make her way in the world—and partly by Hollywood. (She was born in an army barracks, daughter to a sergeant in the lowly East India Company Infantry and was educated in the regiment's garrison school. Her husband was an army pay clerk.)

Anna's achievements are all the more impressive for her impoverished beginnings. After her husband's death she was left penniless and alone in Asia, with two small children to take care of. She started a school in Singapore; soon this brought her to the attention of the Siamese consul, who had been instructed to find an English governess for the King of Siam. Anna moved into the opulence of the Siamese court and into popular history. Given the title "Lord Most Excellent Teacher" at court, with her strongly held views and sense of mission she had an enormous impact: King Chulalongkorn, whom she had taught as a prince, later attributed the abolition of slavery and the introduction of a national education system to her teachings, although he was saddened by her portrayal of his father as a cruel and ridiculous tyrant.

At the age of forty-two, and very much the upright Victorian lady, Anna moved to Halifax to live near relatives. Her presence was immediately felt. For a start, she had no time for imperialism. She never referred to "we British," but always "the British," whom she felt strongly had no right to govern India. She was also deeply resentful of Victorian missionaries who attempted to convince devotees that Christianity offered the only hope of salvation. Having studied Buddhism and other Eastern teachings from the age of sixteen, she was to lecture in Sanskrit and translate Hindu scriptures until her death. (She would be pleased to learn that the city has become the headquarters of an international school of Western Buddhists.)

Her concern for women's rights was clear from the time she had bravely stood up for harem women at the Siamese court. In 1894 the Countess of Aberdeen visited the city to organize a local Council of Women. Anna attended and was able to lend a deep perspective by pointing out that, two thousand years before, women in India had formed a council to enable them to further the welfare of themselves and their children.

Anna's most enduring achievement in Halifax was the founding of the Victoria School of Art and Design, to commemorate the Queen's Golden Jubilee. A century later, as the Nova Scotia College of Art and Design, the school is the only major degree-granting art school in Canada. It has a reputation as the most avant-garde school in the country and is largely responsible for the vitality of the graphic design and jewelry businesses in the city.

Anna
Leonowens in
later years.

said to be the tallest of its kind in the world. This distinguished building is constructed of local ironstone dressed with granite and effortlessly combines its older classical Georgian lines with the Gothic Revival elements introduced in the 1860s. It replaced the wooden St. Peter's Church (1784), which was dismantled, ferried across to Dartmouth, and reassembled there; before St. Peter's, the site had been occupied by the town's first prison. Behind the church is the original location of St. Mary's University (see page 162).

Across and a few metres up Spring Garden Road is the **Old Court House** (1858), situated on the spot where, in 1760, the Micmac buried the hatchet and so made peace with the English settlers. Among many other proceedings, the trial of the ships' crewmen held to be responsible for the Great Explosion of 1917 was held here.

Note on the east side of Barrington Street, at its junction with Spring Garden Road, the two British War Department granite **Survey Markers.** These mark the site of Imperial Military Headquarters until the British departure in 1906, and then of Canadian Military Headquarters until 1917.

Opposite St. Mary's Basilica is the Old Burying Ground.

Old Burying Ground

Originally located outside the old town's log walls, the cemetery was set aside for burials in 1749 and used for those citizens whose eminence did not qualify them for burial under St. Paul's Church. Many gravestones are similar to New England stones of the period, marking the old colony's close ties.

The **Old Burying Ground** also has some remarkable associations with a less fraternal time with the United States. In addition to the remains of many townspeople, the bones of General Ross lie here. After a highly distinguished career fighting Napoleon, this British general went on to burn Washington during the War of 1812, inadvertently giving the United States the symbol of the White House (the pale limestone building of the President's mansion was so badly scorched it had to be painted, white was the colour chosen). He died in the ensuing battle of Baltimore, during which Francis Scott Key wrote the United States national anthem, "The Star Spangled Banner." The general's tombstone may be found to the left of and several metres behind the triumphal arch.

Captain Lawrence of the USS *Chesapeake* was also interred

here after his death in the fight with HMS *Shannon* in the same war. He was laid to rest by a full redcoat guard of honour and later reinterred in Trinity Church, New York. The Captain attained immortality in the United States navy for his uttering of the slogan, "Don't Give Up the Ship," during the encounter with the *Shannon.*

Surmounted by an imperial lion, the triumphal arch behind the gate commemorates the heroic deaths in the Crimean War of two Haligonian officers in British regiments.

On the opposite side of Barrington Street is **St. Matthew's Church** (1859). It was built after the original church—erected in 1754 as a Protestant Dissenting Meeting House—had burned to the ground. The church is little changed from its founding year: the high pulpit is characteristic of early Scottish churches, while the enclosed box pews were originally auctioned to members. The best pews were against the walls and sold for $144 a year; free seats without backs were in the centre. Also of interest is the Rose Window (a copy of the one in Chartres Cathedral), the Old Kirk Fiddle that was used before the organ was installed, and the blue carpet in the Lieutenant-Governor's Pew—a section of the one used in Westminster Abbey at the coronation of Queen Elizabeth II.

Government House

Next to the church is **Government House** (1800), a tangible symbol of one of the town's most celebrated eras and the oldest continuously occupied executive residence in North America. The cornerstone was laid by Prince Edward, the Duke of Kent. When completed, Government House gave a new air of permanence and dignity to the boisterous young colony. The building remains a splendid example of Georgian architecture, reflecting the Palladian style of English country houses of the day.

Built at the urging of Sir John and Lady Frances Wentworth, it replaced the previous Governor's residence (situated where Province House is now). After her earlier close friendship with Prince William and with the brilliant presence in town of Prince Edward, Lady Frances and her husband felt driven towards a mansion befitting their status—the old one, they said, was "in Danger of falling into the Cellar."

It is a remarkable testament to the Wentworths' determination that the new mansion was constructed at all—in the middle of the

SOCIAL LIFE IN THE FORTRESS TOWN

*F*or most of its existence Halifax was a vital stronghold of the Empire, and the daily life of the fortress town reverberated with military activity.

Redcoats and bluejackets were everywhere. Drills and guard mountings were held on the Grand Parade in the centre of town, while bagpipes, brass, and drums resounded up and down the narrow streets. Signal cannon boomed from warships in the harbour and from the Citadel at noon and in the evening, and, for many Haligonians, the final sound of the day was the rich melancholy of the Last Post played from the fort's ramparts.

On Sunday mornings, regimental bands led the garrison through the streets to service at St. Paul's. In the afternoon, until the 1830s, the town flocked to the Common to see the Governor and his imposing suite of officers review the garrison. At dusk, pleasure boats gathered around the great hulls of the warships in the harbour to listen to sailors' sea shanties and the ritual end of day rifle shots. It seemed as if the town could not get enough.

It was a mutual affection. Army and navy, officers and men, all regarded Halifax as the choicest outpost in the Empire. Their regimental histories are full of comments such as "Halifax has been a delightful station and all will be sorry to leave it, the men especially so." For a start, they liked the climate. By contrast, Bermuda was hot and unhealthy, Gibraltar was hot and claustrophobic, Malta was hot and boring, and so on.

The town also offered many distractions. For the men, the off-duty hours provided a respite from fierce discipline and the tedium of guard duty. It usually meant getting stuporously drunk on Water Street, or in taking some momentary delights in the bawdy-houses of Barrack Street, or in the simple pleasures of a brawl with another regiment or with the "other service." The more genteel among them might be able to arrange a gentle flirtation with a scullery maid in the Public Gardens. For the officers, almost all of them members of the aristocracy or the upper classes, Halifax was something of a paradise. They loved the town itself—its quiet and its gaiety—and there was ample entertainment: riding in Point Pleasant Park, playing polo at Fort Needham, yachting in the harbour, skating on the Arm, and, in earlier years, the occasional cockfight. And then, ushered in by the May arrival of the Naval Squadron, there was the annual round of formal balls and garden parties in regimental messes and private estates.

This, in a sense, was just the beginning. Few wealthy Halifax merchants would not want their daughters married to an upper-crust Englishman—the most desirable catch, many thought, in the civilized world. For the young officer it was "an elysium of bliss" and, with the chance of marrying Haligonian money, a profitable prospect: a suitor might be drawn aside by envious rival officers with "Lucky dog! Jolly girl! Nice little piece of ordnance—fifty thousand pounder...."

There was, then, something of a love affair between the townspeople and their defenders. So, when a battalion was to sail home or off to some far-flung colonial battle, half of Halifax went down to the troopships to see them off, while the bands on the quayside played old sentimental tunes such as "The Girl I Left Behind Me" and "Will Ye No Come Back Again." But the replacing regiment with its hundreds of new faces would have arrived, and a fresh round of activity was already under way.

long Napoleonic Wars, in the teeth of fierce opposition from their political adversaries, and at a cost about three times the amount projected (in a colony of sixty thousand people, £30,000 was an enormous cost to bear for a home for the King's Representative). In fact the vice regal pair moved in two years before the building was completed and immediately hosted a series of glittering balls and dinners, setting a standard seldom equalled since.

For almost two hundred years, Government House's links to the monarchy have remained unbroken, and it has hosted a long procession of royal guests, most recently Queen Elizabeth. Among many other visitors, in 1808 Aaron Burr—the former United States Vice-President who shot Alexander Hamilton to death in a duel—unfolded in the mansion a scheme for the British seizure of Florida from the Spanish. (The British declined to participate.)

Government House from the Southwest (Woolford, 1819).

Following a venerable New Year's Day tradition, the Lieutenant-Governor continues to hold a levee to which Haligonians at large are invited, personally greeting everyone as they arrive. In less democratic times, officers and professional people attended the levee one day; tradespeople came the next.

···· *Continue to the corner of Bishop and Barrington Streets.*

On this corner, in 1828 the Stoddard House was built of native ironstone and sandstone as the **Presbyterian Manse.** In the 1880s, the author of Anne of Green Gables, L. M. Montgomery, then a student at Dalhousie University, lived in the corner room under the mansard roof. Note the stone street marker cut into the wall, the last of its kind in the city. Next to the staircase is an old cannon buried muzzle-down to fend off passing carriage wheels, a common practice at the time and perhaps a nineteenth-century echo of the swords-into-ploughshares theme.

This part of Barrington Street used to be known as Pleasant Street, as it continued south to Point Pleasant. It was a favourite walk for townspeople for many years, along which at first they were accompanied by redcoats as protection against Indian attacks.

···· *The curious explorer might like to continue a few blocks further down Barrington Street. If not, turn left down Bishop Street towards the harbour and continue at the hand (☛) below.*

Along Barrington Street are a number of engaging nineteenth-century buildings, specifically at 1349, 1334, 1264, 1253-1259, 1230-1234, and 1222. (To your left—east—down Morris Street is the **Halliburton House,** originally the home of Sir Brenton Halliburton, Chief Justice from 1833.)

Number 1264 (currently the Waverley Inn) was the Waverley Hotel where Oscar Wilde stayed during his visit to Halifax. **Number 1222** (currently the Granite Brewery), built in 1834 and reminiscent of Scottish homes of the period, was the home of William Henry, one of the founding fathers of Confederation.

At the northwest corner of Barrington and South Streets is the **Maritime Command Building.** During the Second World War it was the headquarters for air operations during the Battle of the Atlantic (see page 116–17). Originally the Navy League Building, the foundation stone was laid in 1919 by the Prince of Wales, who later reigned as Edward VIII, until his abdication.

In the square opposite stands the statue of Edward Cornwallis, who in 1749 led the expedition to found Halifax.

···· *Return to the corner of Barrington and Bishop Streets and turn right along Bishop.*
☛ *From Bishop Street turn left along Hollis Street.*

Directly across from Government House on Hollis Street stood, through the Second World War, a bawdy-house of wide repute. The proximity of the King's Representative to a renowned madam gave, as the city historian puts it, "a certain unique distinction to this area during much of the war."

Next, along the right-hand side of the street, is the **Benjamin Wier House** (at 1459), built in 1863 in the style of an Italian villa. During the American Civil War, Wier, who championed the Confederate cause, was involved in the risky business of blockade-running into the southern ports. He provisioned the Confederate raider *Tallahassee* before her daring escape from Union warships down the harbour's Eastern Channel.

Keith Hall
Hollis Street
(L. B.
Jenson).

Also involved in the *Tallahassee*'s escape was the brewer Alexander Keith, who lived next door to Wier in his Italian Renaissance style home, called **Keith Hall** (at 1475), also built in 1863. Inside the house the palazzo motif is continued, with marble fireplaces and elaborate woodwork and mouldings. The sandstone building is, unfortunately, deteriorating.

Across the street, next to Government House, is the **Black-Binney House.** Faced with granite from Aberdeenshire in Scotland, it was built around 1820 for John Black, a successful merchant and privateer (he owned the Caledonia, the first vessel to be commissioned for privateering in the War of 1812). The building was later owned by the Right Reverend Hibbert Binney, the Anglican bishop of Nova Scotia. A strong-willed man, he relished heated ecclesiastical debate and socializing in equal measure. The building is now the local headquarters of the Canadian Corps of Commissionaires.

As you continue north along Hollis to Salter Street, you can see **Keith's Brewery** on the right. (It is best seen from the Salter Street entrance or from Water Street.) Constructed in 1837 of native ironstone, the brewery produced beer here until 1971, continuing even during Prohibition—for export only. During the VE Day Riots in 1945 it was a main focus of the mob's attention.

The building has been converted for use as shops, restaurants, and offices. A visit to the inner courtyard provides both a good opportunity for some midtour refreshment and a view of the courtyard with its intriguingly churchlike Victorian windows. Saturdays, when the **Farmer's Market** is held here, are ideal for a visit.

···· *Return to Hollis Street and proceed one block north along Hollis, past Sackville Street.*

On the right-hand side of the street, from number 1659 to the next corner is **Founder's Square,** a redevelopment project incorporating eight buildings of striking historical interest. At one time or another fourteen newspaper offices were located here, from those of small scandal-sheets to the office of Howe's mighty newspaper, the *Novascotian*. Built between 1816 and 1867, they represent a spectrum of architectural styles.

Number 1663 (between 1659 and 1667) is the old **Lenoir Building,** built about 1816 for the Lenoir family who lived here for over sixty years. It is associated with François Truffaut's film, *The Story of Adele H.*, which records the tragic story of the daughter of French novelist Victor Hugo and her impassioned pursuit of a British Army lieutenant stationed in Halifax, when her friend and confidant was Peter Lenoir. Adele dogged the lieutenant's steps for three years and, after he married a Dartmouth girl, went insane.

On the left-hand side of the street, at **1674,** a typical Georgian building of the time, was built in 1828 as a merchant's shop with the residence above. Among the long succession of tenants, in 1862 the London Drug Store occupied the building and dispensed such Victorian bromides as Langley's Cordial Rhubarb, Cockle's Antibilious Pills, and Leeming's Essence for Lameness in Horses.

Next door, at 1682, is the **Halifax Club.** Constructed in 1862, it stands as a monument to the town's affluence acquired from shipbuilding and trade in the age of sail. Patterned after London clubs, this colonial version with its Italian Renaissance styling is as full of consequence as any in the mother country—complete with a prohibition against women members, only recently lifted. Before their respective accessions to the throne, Kings Edward VII and George V were feted at dinners in the club. In less glamorous times, commanders of merchant convoys during the Second World War were made welcome here.

As you reach the corner of Hollis and Prince Streets, to your right on Prince (at 5140, the third building down) is the **Novascotian Building.** From these premises Joseph Howe published his newspaper.

···· *Cross Prince Street to Province House, which is on your left.*

S H O R T   T O U R   Continue from this point.

Province House

Open to visitors throughout the year, between July 1 and Labour Day Province House offers guided tours seven days a week, 8:30 A.M.– 6:00 P.M. (shorter hours on the weekend). Free admission.

Completed in 1819, **Province House** is the oldest British colonial parliament building in the world and the finest Georgian building in Canada. In 1842, Charles Dickens called it "a gem of

Georgian architecture," and later judgements have warmly supported his view. The scene of historic political events, it has also hosted a variety of other occasions, including visits from a long procession of Royals. In more recent times it has been the home of the Nova Scotia Legislature.

Province House had an arduous birth. As early as 1787 the authorities had passed an Act to begin building. When no progress had been made ten years later, they passed a new Act to speed things up, only to be blocked by Sir John and Lady Frances Wentworth, whose wish for a new Government House had become overwhelming. Once completed, the cost of the latter so stunned the town, it was not until 1811 that the cornerstone was laid for Province House. Work went slowly through lack of funds, and the building was finally finished eight years later—thirty-two years after the original Act had been passed.

Province House (Wilkie, 1854).

No doubt remembering the Government House expense, the authorities hired no architect for Province House. It was designed by a local contractor of paints and varnishes to the military, John Merrick, and supervised by a stonemason.

With all this, it is a small wonder that the building is as distinguished as it is. Merrick's inspired design includes features of the

Palladian style, popular in England in the late eighteenth and early nineteenth centuries, visible in the rusticated stonework of the ground floor and the Ionic pillars surmounted by triangular pediments. The Royal Crest holds pride of place in the central pediment.

···· *Entering Province House from Hollis Street, proceed up the stairs to the second floor.*

To your right is the **Red Chamber,** the home of the Legislative Council until 1928. For the first century after Halifax's founding the Governor and his Council wielded autocratic power and for the last few decades of their reign met in this room. In the centre of the room is the **Beaufort Table,** perhaps the most historically significant piece of furniture in Canada. In 1749 on the ship *Beaufort,* Cornwallis and his Council met around this table to plan the infant town and colony. More recently, the cabinet of the provincial government has met around it to design Nova Scotia's future. On the dais at the end of the chamber are two red chairs, reserved for the British monarch and consort. The original chair was built in 1860 for the Prince of Wales's visit; the other chair was speedily copied from the original for Queen Elizabeth (the Queen Mother) when she visited the town with King George VI in 1939. Only the style of crown on the seat back distinguishes one from the other.

On the walls are portraits of British monarchs and distinguished Nova Scotians, including John Inglis, the hero of the Siege of Lucknow during the Indian Mutiny, and Thomas Chandler Haliburton, eminent jurist and creator of Sam Slick, one of the first humorous characters in North American fiction. Note, too, the wealth of detail and symbol included in the scrollwork and plasterwork in the room.

Among the many events held in the Red Chamber, in 1856 the city welcomed back its veterans from the Crimean War with a ball for the officers of the 62nd Regiment. The event was illuminated by the new-fangled gas jets spelling out such slogans as "SEBASTOPOL" and "HONOUR TO THE BRAVE," requiring the special attendance throughout the evening of the city fire department.

Leaving the Red Chamber, on your right is the **Legislative Library,** once the chamber used by the law courts. It is the room in which the most celebrated event in Nova Scotian political history occurred. In March 1835, with the room crammed to overflowing, Joseph Howe brilliantly defended himself against charges of libel brought by the magistrates, striking a mighty blow for freedom of speech. So began the dismantling of the autocratic power of the Governor and his Council.

In 1819 the chamber was the scene of the trial of Richard John Uniacke, Jr., by his father, the Attorney General, for killing a man in a duel. Acquitted of the charge of murder (at that time duelling was still an affair of honour) the younger Uniacke apparently never recovered from the experience and died at an early age.

As you leave the library, the **Assembly Chamber** is to your right. When the Legislative Assembly is in session, you may view the proceedings from the **Visitors' Gallery**, approached up the flight of stairs opposite the library; during the summer months you may visit the chamber itself, accompanied by a House guide.

The Assembly Chamber echoes the main elements of the Mother of Parliaments in Westminster in a dignified colonial style and on a smaller scale—Charles Dickens remarked that "it was like looking at Westminster through the wrong end of a telescope." The **Speaker's Chair** dominates the seats of the Government on his right and of the Opposition on his left; to the left of the chair is a portrait of Joseph Howe. In the centre of the chamber is the mace carried by the Sergeant-at-Arms, which represents the authority of the monarch.

The upper gallery windows are bordered with a variety of motifs, including falcons. Note that several of these birds have been decapitated: during a period of anti-American feeling in the 1840s, a member of the Assembly, in a rush of blood to the head, was reminded of the American eagle and went about bludgeoning the wooden birds with his cane.

As you leave Province House by the Hollis Street entrance, note the pair of lamp standards next to the stairs. As if to officially stamp the solid Britishness of the building and its allegiances, the standards are from London's old Waterloo Bridge.

At the south end of the building is the **Joseph Howe Statue**, gesturing towards both the Novascotian Building, the home of Howe's newspaper, and towards Britain, to which he was so loyal. Flanking the building are two cannon. The one at the north end is a 32-pounder, reputedly from HMS *Shannon,* which captured the USS *Chesapeake* in 1813. This cannon was used up to 1905 as the town's noon gun.

JOSEPH HOWE: A GREAT NOVA SCOTIAN

*H*e has been called "the voice of Nova Scotia," "Nova Scotia's Tribune," an "Empire-builder," a great orator, and a superb writer. Some have seen him as headstrong and ambitious. But all who met him agree that Joseph Howe left a powerful impression. A man of immense warmth, at ease with everyone—he was talked of admiringly as the man who had kissed every woman in Nova Scotia—he found a direct path to most people's affections.

Born in 1804 in a cottage on the Northwest Arm, young Joe found an early love for his native land—matched only by a passionate loyalty to the Empire. Although he had few opportunities for schooling, he read widely, and after a brief apprenticeship, at the age of twenty-three bought himself a newspaper, the *Novascotian*. Combining a vigorous curiosity about people and their affairs with his need to collect subscription money, he travelled widely in the colony. All the while he polished his formidable writing skills.

In 1835 his growing concern at the misrule of the colony thrust him to centre stage. He attacked the autocratic rule of the Governor and his Council, accusing the magistrates appointed by them of corruption. He was charged with libel, and defending himself in Province House, he won over the jury by flaming oratory in which he called the magistrates "the most negligent and imbecile ... body that ever mismanaged a people's affairs." His acquittal caused an uproar in the town: all recognized that he had won a great victory for freedom of speech.

To advance the quest for Responsible Government, Howe became the leader of the Reformers. Although his loyalty to the Crown never wavered (he said, "We seek for nothing more than British subjects are entitled to"), he campaigned tirelessly against the "dictatorial style" of British rule.

Meanwhile, his fiery pen provoked more and more resentment from those in power, and in 1840 he was forced to fight a duel against the son of a judge whose honour he was felt to have impugned. One Governor said that between Howe and himself it was a "war to the knife." Finally, in 1848 Responsible Government— elected government responsible to the people—was granted to Nova Scotia. It was the first such government in any colony in the Empire.

After this great triumph, Howe's vision and ambition expanded. Foreshadowing today's Commonwealth, he proposed a great imperial federation of all the British colonies, in which he hoped to play an eminent role. An advocate of the intercolonial railway, he was responsible for the building of the Nova Scotian railways. Ever loyal to the Empire, during the Crimean War he travelled to the United States to seek recruits for the British forces, barely escaping with his life when an angry anti-British mob surrounded his New York hotel.

Joseph Howe carried in triumph down the steps of Province House (Jeffreys).

In the 1860s, as Britain's North American colonies moved towards confederation, Howe at first strongly opposed the scheme. He felt that it would not work and—more importantly—that Nova Scotians had not been adequately consulted. But Her Majesty's Government was determined: Nova Scotia became part of the Dominion of Canada. Saddened by Britain's seeming contempt for Nova Scotia's interests, he did his utmost to gain the best possible terms for the new province.

In May 1873, Howe was appointed Lieutenant-Governor of Nova Scotia by the Dominion whose creation he had opposed. He moved into Government House and three weeks later, exhausted by his efforts, died.

At the north end of the building is the slightly quixotic **Boer War Monument.** The soldier is signalling with his rifle, "Enemy in Sight" (a stance which in that and later wars may well have been his last). The foundation stone was laid in 1901 by George V as Duke of York; his "consort" was crowned Queen Mary. The monument stands on the site of Cornwallis's 1749 house—"a bare musket shot from the waterside"—which was used by Governors until it had become surrounded by rum taverns, fish shops, and disreputability, when the current Government House was built.

···· *Cross Hollis Street at the northern end of Province House.*

On the corner of Hollis and George Streets is the **Old Post Office** building (currently the home of the Art Gallery of Nova Scotia). Started in the flush of the province's prosperity in 1863, such was the strength of the town's anti-Confederation sentiment after 1867 that the provincial government initially refused to hand the building over to the new Dominion. Still dominated by the robust 4 m (12 ft.) statue of Britannia on the pediment, but missing its original domed clock tower, the building has been used as a post office, customs house, and law courts. Until quite recently, it was the headquarters of the Royal Canadian Mounted Police.

The **Art Gallery of Nova Scotia** is now housed in the thoroughly renovated building. Mandated to preserve regional culture, the gallery has about two thousand works in its collection, including many of absorbing historical interest as well as more recent folk art. Canadian, British, and European painting are well represented. The gallery also periodically presents its special collection.

The gallery is open year-round from 10:00 A.M. (Sundays from noon); it is closed on Mondays and holidays. Small admission charge (none on Tuesdays). Telephone (902)424-7542 for further information.

The open area directly in front of the Old Post Office building, between Hollis and Bedford Row, is Cheapside. From the mid-nineteenth century up to 1917 it was the site of a colourful and widely known open air market; here Micmac, Acadians, blacks, and fishermen sold their wares from baskets, stalls, and from the backs of wagons.

Take the stairs from Cheapside down to Bedford Row and turn right on Bedford Row towards Prince Street.

From the corner of Bedford Row and Prince Street is a fine view of the Founder's Square buildings, particularly the Novascotian Building, the second one from the near corner.

···· *Turn left down Prince Street to Water Street.*

On the southwest corner is the **Mitchell Building**, the last of its kind on the old waterfront. Constructed around 1830 for the Mitchell family, who were West India merchants, the ironstone building was used by them both as a residence and as a warehouse. It was built near their wharf at the end of Prince Street. (In the nineteenth century merchants frequently built their homes on Water Street, close to where their ships came in.)

···· *Cross Water Street, turn right and proceed a few yards to the Maritime Museum of the Atlantic.*

The **Maritime Museum of the Atlantic** offers a compelling view into Nova Scotia's rich maritime history, while the nearby wharves are good vantage points from which to survey the harbour. Housed in a former ship chandlery and warehouse dating from the 1870s, with a modern exhibition hall attached, the museum offers a variety of displays. Ships are well represented, ranging from a large model collection to full-sized craft, including local dories and Gundalows, and the elegantly carved Royal Barge used by Queen Victoria (presented to her on her Golden Jubilee in 1887). Moored at the museum's wharf is the CSS *Acadia,* a hydrographic survey ship built in 1913. There are also permanent displays on the age of steam, an engrossing exhibit on Nova Scotia's halcyon days—the age of sail—and a well-stocked nineteenth-century ship chandlery in its original premises, redolent with the smells of rope and tar.

The museum is open year-round; closed Mondays between October 15 and June 1 (shorter hours on Sundays.). Free admission in off-season (October 15–June 1); small admission in summer. Call (902)424-7490.

The World War II corvette **HMCS *Sackville*** is moored near the museum during the extended summer season. Open to visitors, this impeccably restored ship is the last remaining example of more than a hundred built by the Royal Canadian Navy to counter the U-boat threat in the Atlantic. In August 1942 she was

Samuel Cunard: Steamship Pioneer

*I*n 1787 Samuel Cunard was born in a small house on Brunswick Street. From these modest surroundings, he made a vast contribution to the nineteenth century by his advancement of steamship travel and assembled a large fortune. His name was to become a household word.

One of Philadelphia's leading families, the Cunards entered the shipping business after the discovery—so family legend had it—of pirates' loot on their land. But the family were British Loyalists, and in the aftermath of the American Revolution their property was confiscated. They left for Nova Scotia. Things again began to go their way when, during the War of 1812, they acquired a captured American square-rigger at a rock-bottom price and began to use the ship for trading.

Determined to restore the family's fortune, young Sam, "a bright, tight little man with keen eyes, firm lips and a happy manner," became known as a sharp but reliable business-man. Over the years he traded in a dizzying variety of com-modities, including tea, coffee, and coal. He married a local girl and became active in the town: among his many duties, he headed the Lighthouse Commission of Nova Scotia and was colonel of the Scarlet Runners, a militia regiment noted for its red coats.

He also became friendly with Joseph Howe. Both men were patriots, both were imperially minded—Sam had hero-worshipped the godlike figure of the Duke of Kent—and both saw the immense possibilities of the new steamboats for ocean travel, with Halifax as the main Western terminus. Howe encouraged Cunard to tender for the transatlantic mail contract, which he won.

In July 1840 he began his service to Halifax and Boston with the steamer *Britannia*. Now nothing could hold him back. From the beginning he emphasized dependability rather than luxury or speed. In the early years at least, this may have been a bit overdone: travelling to North America on the *Britannia* in 1842, Charles Dickens declared his cabin to be a "a profoundly preposterous box;" as for the bunk, "nothing smaller for sleeping in was ever made, except coffins."

But the Cunard line soon earned an unequalled reputation for reliability as travellers came to trust the new ships. The popularity of steamship travel blossomed, opening the way for the mass immigrations to the New World and for the great expansion of the British Empire.

Over two centuries, Cunard's ships have, as one historian put it, given "an unprecedented impetus to commerce, and have rendered inestimable service to the people of every country." They also served the Empire in wartime. During the Crimean War, Cunard ordered fourteen vessels converted to war transports; for this he was knighted in 1859. The tradition continued: Among many other vessels, the legendary Cunard liners *Queen Elizabeth* and *Queen Mary* served as fast troop transports in the Second World War, the latter bringing Winston Churchill to Halifax in 1943.

Today, one and a half centuries after the *Britannia* sailed into the harbour, Cunard's *Queen Elizabeth 2*—which in turn served in the Falklands War—plies the seas, regularly calling at Halifax. The vessel has been described as "probably the most beautiful, powerful and efficient passenger ship of all time."

....

responsible for seriously damaging one U-boat, hitting another with her four-inch guns, and badly shaking up a third with depth charges.

The HMCS *Sackville* Interpretive Centre, next to the museum, gives a captivating sense of the ship and her times.

In those dark years the harbour was filled with warships and merchant vessels struggling to keep open the lifeline to an embattled Britain; it had become the most important harbour in the world. At various times it has certainly been the most important seaport in North America. From D'Anville's doomed expedition and the later British fleets bound for the capture of Louisbourg, Quebec, and Canada in the mid-eighteenth century to the large and hugely profitable merchant fleets of the nineteenth century, and its crucial importance in the two world wars, the harbour has played a central historical role.

To further explore the harbour front, continue south—to your right from the museum—along the boardwalk, where you can see the harbour's tugboat fleet at its wharves. If you are interested in maritime naval history, be sure to visit the Maritime Command Museum on Gottingen Street.

···· *On leaving the museum, turn right on Water Street and walk past the end of George Street to the Ferry Terminal.*

For much of the city's history, the many wharves and shipping businesses located along **Water Street** made it a hive of activity. The area was a forest of tall masts and rigging, and seamen from the four corners of the world made their loud ways to and from its taverns—from the settlement's earliest days the street was lined with shacks and drinking dens, to become known as "The Beach." In the 1750s, stocks and a gallows were located on Water Street at the bottom of George Street, thoughtfully located as a warning to arriving seamen, soldiers, and colonists.

To your right is the **Dartmouth ferry**, the oldest operating saltwater ferry service in North America and an irresistible bargain of a side trip across the harbour and back. It began operating in 1752, using a "team-boat"—seven or eight horses harnessed to a rotating windlass on the deck—until the introduction of a paddle steamer in 1830.

···· *Continue along Water Street—a few minutes' walk—to Historic Properties.*

Historic Properties

Just past the entrance to the shopping mall, the broad alley to the right leads to the **Historic Properties** buildings. In the 1970s this group of historic buildings—the only remaining waterfront examples of Halifax's rough and colourful past—was rescued from developers' bulldozers by a group of concerned and spirited citizens and is now a National Historic Site.

To your immediate right is the ironstone **Pickford & Black Building**. Built around 1830, it was used by the Pickford & Black Company as offices for their shipping agent and steamship business and as a ship chandlery. As recently as the 1960s it held artefacts typical of the Victorian shipping office: large leather-topped partners' desks, wood panelling, tiled fireplaces, and the like.

On your left is the **Collins Bank**, the oldest bank building in Canada. It was built in 1823 by Captain Enos Collins who had made an early fortune from his legendary ship, the *Liverpool Packet;* the ship was a one-time slaver that he converted into a privateer, and with which he terrorized the New England coast during the War of 1812. With the riches gained from these ventures, Collins became a powerful figure and was invited to join the Council of Twelve. With the Governor, the Council held in their hands the power and wealth of the colony—for a while Collins Bank held a complete monopoly. As the Honourable Enos Collins and founder of the local YMCA, he died reputedly the richest man in Canada.

Beyond the bank is the **Old Red Store**, built in 1810 and used as an auction house for prizes captured from American vessels by Nova Scotian privateers during the War of 1812. In later years it served as the British War Department Offices and, more recently, as a seaman's chapel. Today it is Information Centre for the Nova Scotian Department of Tourism, a valuable resource for excursions in the province. The slip adjoining the store is currently the berth of *Bluenose II,* a precise replica of the famous racing schooner *Bluenose.* When the vessel is at her berth or steering into the harbour, the days of sail become tangible.

The ironstone **Privateers' Warehouse,** between the bank and the store, was used to store privateers' captured goods before auction. At the end of the warehouse is the Wooden Store and Sail Loft, built in the 1870s with loose floorboards, so that during exceptionally high tides the boards would float free, decreasing the chance of damage to the structure.

···· *Return to Water Street.*

Across the street to your right is the old **Morse's Tea Building** (1841). Constructed of granite-trimmed ironstone, it gives a strong sense of the Dickensian quality of the waterfront area in the last century and for much of the current one. The site was previously occupied by an elegant and elaborate eighteenth-century building that housed the Jerusalem Coffee House.

···· *Turn left along Water Street to the corner of Duke Street.*

The red brick building on the corner is the site of the Great Pontac, the most popular inn and tavern during the first decades of the town's existence. It saw many sparkling and uproarious gatherings, the most notable of which may have been the dinner given by General James Wolfe before he set off on the expedition to take the Fortress of Louisbourg. The tavern was situated next to a small cove, and on occasion captains of the Royal Navy would have their ship's cook prepare special dishes on board, to be rushed across the harbour in a longboat and delivered piping hot to the tavern's table.

···· *Cross the street and proceed two blocks up Duke Street to Granville Street.*

To your right on **Granville Street** is a streetscape of unusual architectural significance. The buildings on both sides of the Promenade display a graceful assortment of Victorian styles unique in North America and have been masterfully restored as part of the Historic Properties project. When completed in 1859–60, they housed the most fashionable stores in the Maritimes, replacing an equally elegant set of wooden buildings destroyed by fire in 1859. The nineteenth-century horse troughs in the Promenade are original, moved here from other parts of the city. The lanterns are accurate replicas of those which illuminated the street after 1859.

On the building at the northwest corner of Duke and Granville Streets is the coat of arms of the Prince of Wales. When he visited Halifax in 1860, the Prince—Queen Victoria's son and the future Edward VII—amiably granted the request of a local shop owner to place his arms on the merchant's new store.

···· *Continue up Duke Street and turn left on Barrington to return to the Grand Parade.*

On the corner of Duke and Barrington Streets, at the back of the City Hall, is the **Halifax Tourism Visitor Information Bureau.** Open during the summer months, it provides helpful information for visitors on city events, harbour tours, and so on.

Citadel Hill

Tour 2 covers Citadel Hill, which has been a favourite vantage point for Haligonians since their town's birth and offers a striking panorama of the city, its harbour, and the outlying islands. On its crown is the Citadel, one of the finest remaining examples of a nineteenth-century bastioned fort and Canada's most frequently visited historic site. Just below it is the Old Town Clock, Halifax's celebrated landmark.

The only battle ever fought over the hill occurred in the 1970s, when concerned citizens rallied to stem the onrush of high-rises. After fourteen years' skirmishing, the city passed amendments that preserved view planes and limited the height of buildings around the hill; the view remains impressive.

Halifax from the Citadel (Canadian Illustrated News, 1877).

Introduction
Note: Tour 2 begins on page 83.

Old Town Clock
Like the town itself, this simple and beguiling structure was born of military need. Prince Edward, the Duke of Kent, had a

reputation as a fearsome disciplinarian and—determined that the troops under his command would have no excuse for lateness—he made sure that the work found a place in his ambitious Halifax building programme. He personally ordered the clock mechanism from the Royal clockmakers. When the structure was finished in October 1803, his successor as Commander-in-Chief

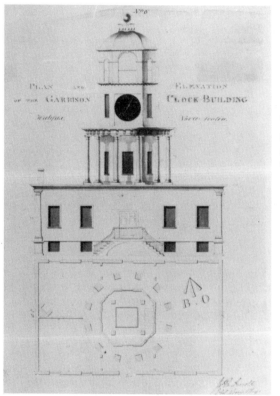

Town Clock, front elevation (Arnold, 1823).
....

carried through the full spirit of the Duke's intent in his General Orders: "The Erection of the Garrison Clock being completed, the Parades and Other Duties are in future to be regulated by it."

The Duke had originally intended the work to be the garrison clock for a barracks situated below the north end of the hill. But the city fathers had other ideas. Forty years before they had voted £50 towards a clock which had never been built and—seeing their opportunity after the Duke's departure—Lieutenant-Governor Sir

John Wentworth persuaded the military to erect the clock in a place where both soldier and civilian could see it.

In the end, it was very much a joint project. Workers from the town completed the rectangular building at the base, while the British Army built the turret. The copper sheathing for the dome—originally intended for the hulls of His Majesty's warships—was supplied from Naval Stores.

When the British military left Halifax in 1906, they gave the city the right to "use and occupy" the building. The city in turn gave up this right to the Crown in 1952 and the clock is now in the care of Parks Canada, which in 1960 extensively restored the building.

The Citadel

Guarding the Royal Navy's dockyard and the town against possible attack by land or sea, from its earliest days the Halifax Citadel was a forceful symbol of British imperial resolve. Long after its usefulness as a fort had ended, it would still proudly fly the Union Jack.

It has been garrisoned by some of the most illustrious British regiments: the Royal Artillery, the 78th Highlanders, the Rifle Brigade, the Green Howards, and the Seaforth Highlanders—among many others—have paraded behind the fortress ramparts.

The current Citadel was preceded on the crown of the hill by three earlier forts. These were built of logs and earth, and while they were strong defences for the day, they were very vulnerable to the climate. The *first Citadel* was one of five small stockaded forts linked by log palisades built around the first settlement to fend off attacks by the Indians and "Canadians" (the French). The *second Citadel* was built around the time of the American Revolution and consisted of a wooden blockhouse surrounded by irregular earthworks that meandered around the slopes (see plan, page 29). Prince Edward built the *third Citadel* as a defence against possible French attacks after the French Revolution, naming it Fort George, after the King. Its design was similar to the present one.

Models of the second, third, and fourth Citadels may be seen in a casemate in the Southeast Salient at the Citadel.

The Duke of Wellington's Commission

In 1825 the Duke of Wellington, Master General of the Board of Ordnance, sent a commission to Canada to survey the defences. They reported that, after years of effort and the expenditure of over £300,000 on the three earlier forts, there was "nothing on Citadel Hill but a heap of ruins."

Realizing that His Majesty's Government's reluctance to fund defences in peacetime was at the root of the problem, the commission recommended spending the money to make the fort permanent. The Commanding Royal Engineer in Halifax, Colonel Gustavus Nicholls, was instructed to draw up plans for a masonry fort.

Nicholls's task was a difficult one. In spite of its commanding presence, the hill was not the perfect site for a fort. For a start, the hill was too far from the shoreline for the fort's smooth-bore cannon to be of much help in the defence of the harbour. Also, the crown of the hill was narrow, making it difficult to construct a fort big enough to be worth the effort; and Camp Hill to the southwest was almost as high and could be a serious threat from an enemy if captured. These were real problems; in 1824 one Royal Engineer wrote: "Every Officer who has been here seems almost to have given the case up in despair."

Building the Fort

The Citadel's chief role was to defend the dockyard and town against overland attacks, either by troops landed from ships that had forced their way up the Northwest Arm or from troops landed in St. Margaret's Bay. (It was expected that the Royal Navy and the Halifax sea batteries would provide an invincible defence against attacks from the sea.) The Citadel was also to be designed as the impregnable keep and strongpoint for the entire fortress system.

In spite of the difficulties presented by the hill, within a few months Nicholls had drafted his plans and sent them to London for approval. As with most forts of the day, his design was influenced by the theories of the seventeenth-century master of siege craft, the Marshal de Vauban. A glance at the main features of the final plan gives us a rich sense of that bygone art of fortifications (see also plan on page 86):

- Ravelins, triangular self-contained forts, helped to solve the problem of the short south and north fronts caused by the

COLONELS, CRICKETERS AND COWS

On the whole it was a good match. The town gained income and security from the military presence, while the military had their base and supplies were provided by the town. And there was real fondness between the townspeople and their soldiers and sailors

But there were always points of friction. For the townspeople, the daily sight of drunken soldiers and sailors roaming the streets, with all the accompanying mischief and mayhem—to say nothing about the occasional riot—was wearing.

It was also irritating that the military seemed to occupy superior sites all over town. The nineteenth-century town historian complained bitterly about the narrow blocks and small lots: "Those whose duty it was to plan and lay out the town appear to have been guided more with a view to the construction of a military encampment than that of a town for the accommodation of an increasing population." Much of the time, as Thomas Raddall has said, it seemed as if, to the military, "the civilians were interlopers."

The military presence was sometimes almost intolerable. Townspeople had to open their windows in all weathers to save them from the concussion of signal and practice cannon, and at least one ricocheting shell landed in a private home. In 1859 the Halifax Cricket Club on the North Common applied to erect a building on their grounds, but the military said it would interfere with their gunners' field of fire from the Citadel. For the same reason, they wouldn't let the town build walls in the general area of the fort.

The irritation was often mutual. In the 1850s the military watched in shocked disbelief as the city lowered Barrack (now Brunswick) Street by 15 ft.—thereby creating a high bank that would give excellent cover to large numbers of enemy troops deploying to attack the Citadel. One nineteenth-century colonel of Royal Engineers may have been pushed over the edge: he became obsessed by invading townspeople and in particular with the cunning psychology of cows, reporting, "I have seen a cow take the railing around the Citadel at a clean bound—cleverly." A short while later he was posted elsewhere.

In April 1877 Lieutenant-General O'Grady Haly came close to provoking an international incident. The young Dominion's Intercolonial Railway was being pushed along the harbour dangerously close to the army's Wellington Barracks with its two magazines, each of which held thirty-five hundred barrels of gunpowder. One of the magazines had blown up twenty years before, and the general was becoming very nervous about the steam engines that were dropping "large red hot cinders" in their neighbourhood.

Frustrated by the fruitless negotiations, the general declared war. He informed Ottawa that his soldiers would seize the railway the following day unless progress was halted. This thunderbolt generated frantic telegrams to London and Halifax, delaying the railway's construction until safer arrangements could be made. So, for another forty years, disaster was averted.

narrowness of the hill and also provided greater protection on the west or landward front.

- Demi-bastions, bastions with three rather than four sides, were placed at the northwest and southwest corners.
- A redan, or V-shaped projection, was located on the harbour side.
- A Cavalier Building, mounting cannon on its roof and providing secure barracks and storage space, was located on the western side of the parade square.

These elements were designed to cover each other, providing overlapping fields of fire in all directions. The final plan of the fort—with its demi-bastions, a ravelin, and the Cavalier Building all placed on the western front—reflected the view that an attack on the Citadel would come from the landward side.

It took three years for Nicholls's plans to make their way through the tottering bureaucracy of the Board of Ordnance in London. But this was only the beginning of the delays in completing the fort.

In an attempt to please the tightfisted authorities in London, Nicholls built the ironstone and granite walls holding the ramparts about 2 ft. thinner than recommended by the Marshal de Vauban. In 1830 large sections of the completed walls in both demi-bastions collapsed; Nicholls reported that he had "made a little too free with the Climate." There was no alternative but to pull the existing construction down and begin again.

This situation and a seemingly endless stream of less spectacular problems—leaking casemates, tugs of war with other commanders over the use of manpower, and so on—caused repeated delays. By the time the fort was ready for its guns in 1853 the cost, originally projected at £116,000, had more than doubled to £242,000, and the work that was to have taken six years to complete had taken over a quarter of a century.

The Garrison

A regiment served two years in the garrison before moving on to the next point in the imperial rotation, which consisted of the Mediterranean, Bermuda, Halifax, the West Indies, and the Cape of Good Hope, concluding with six years in India. Over Halifax's long history almost every British Regiment of the Line served in the fort at least once.

The redcoated troops brought with them both the direct sense of allegiance to the mother country and the rich romanticism of

the imperial vision. Many had served "in the snowy trenches
before Sebastopol, across the hot African sands of Tel-el-Kebir
and up the wooded slopes of the Peiwar Kotal on the North West
Frontier of India." Some had powerful associations with the town
itself: the Lancashire Fusiliers recalled the glory of former members like Wolfe, the conqueror of Quebec; Ross, who·captured
Washington in the War of 1812; and Cornwallis, the founder of
Halifax itself.

But of the many imperial regiments that garrisoned the
Citadel, two are of special importance—the Royal Artillery and
the 78th Highlanders. (Both regiments are represented there
today by students expertly trained in the drill of the 1860s.)

The Royal Regiment of Artillery, unlike the infantry regiments,
served the garrison from the town's founding to the British
departure, manning the guns for one and a half centuries. Two
batteries (about 250 men) were usually assigned to Halifax. The
regiment was prominent in most British campaigns—their motto
was *Ubique* ("Everywhere")—including Louisbourg and Quebec,
and in 1815 they became the toast of Europe for their role in the
Battle of Waterloo.

The 78th Highlanders—also known as the Ross-shire Buffs—
were already emblazoned with military glory when they arrived

....

Regimental
Officers, 78th
Highlanders
(1869).

in May 1869. Under General Arthur Wellesley (later the Duke of Wellington) at the Battle of Assaye in 1803, they had been part of a force that sent an army five times as large into headlong retreat. Fifty years later, the regiment gathered no fewer than six Victoria Crosses fighting to relieve Lucknow, to be immortalized in "The Defence of Lucknow," a poem by Alfred Lord Tennyson.

Some of the regiment were quartered in the Citadel casemates which at the time could accommodate 340 men; the rest were in Wellington Barracks (see page 00) and in detachments around the town. They were a highly popular regiment, partly for their battle record and partly for their bare knees, which in that Victorian age caused a sensation. When they left for home at the end of their duty, Haligonians lined the streets in pouring rain to bid them farewell.

Life for the troops in the fort—and indeed in any British military barracks of the time—was bleak. Quite apart from the abysmal pay and the fierce discipline (flogging was routinely administered for drunkenness), living conditions were cramped and spartan. The issuing of coal to the troops, for example, was strictly controlled; the winter temperature in the damp and often leaky casemates rarely exceeded a chilly 50°F. It lends some perspective on the soldierly life of the time to realize that Halifax was the most sought-after station in the Empire.

During a siege, conditions would be far worse. The military planners estimated that the fort would require a garrison of 1,360 to withstand a six-week siege, composed of 900 infantry (one soldier for every 2 ft. of rampart), 340 artillery, and 120 sappers, who would be used primarily to destroy any tunnels the enemy dug under the glacis.

This was three times the number needed at any one time (to offset casualties and to make it possible to relieve exhausted men) and approximately four times the usual num-

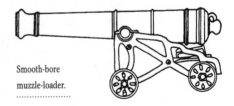

Smooth-bore
muzzle-loader.
....

ber. In addition, it was likely that townspeople would crowd into the fort for protection in the event of an attack. The garrison was, fortunately, never required to undergo the experience.

To arm the fort, Nicholls had proposed a variety of smooth-bore cannon, sixty-seven pieces in all. There were to be twenty-eight 24-pounder guns mounted on the ramparts and the Cavalier, with thirty-five 24-pounder short-barrelled carronades to go into the defence casemates to command the fort's ditches. In addition, he recommended four 13-inch mortars for close-in plunging fire. Long after Nicholls had left the scene, in 1846 the Board of Ordnance approved a plan to increase the armament to ninety-four guns, including the heavier and longer-range 32-pounder

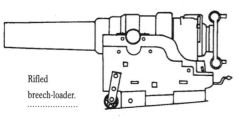

Rifled breech-loader.

cannon. This was the complement of weapons (along with a 12-pounder signal gun) that was finally mounted in 1854—thirty years after Nicholls had sent his plans to London.

Changing Roles

When it was finally completed, the fort was a powerful one. Yet, within three years of the its arming, the advent of the far more powerful rifled guns had made both the armament and the Citadel's planned role obsolete. Its smooth-bore cannon—basically unchanged for three hundred years—were utterly outclassed by the new weapons, while the fort's ironstone and granite walls would be rapidly breached by them.

This radical development made Halifax's outer sea batteries far more vital: an enemy had now to be stopped far out in the harbour approaches. Nevertheless, ambitious plans were laid to modernise the Citadel's armaments—as many as forty-eight rifled guns were recommended. But there was a gradual decline in the number of its weapons from the high point of 1855, and by 1879 only seventeen guns (including eleven rifled muzzle-loaders) were mounted—and these were all on the seaward front. The originally heavily gunned western front had no weapons at all.

So the Citadel, once the centrepiece of the Halifax defences, quietly took its place as just another sea battery, and by no means the most important.

The fort's role, however, continued well into the twentieth century. After the British withdrawal, it served as an administrative centre for Canadian forces, and in both world wars it

WARTIME NIGHTS

*T*hroughout Halifax's history, the outbreak of war was followed by an influx of fighting men and their equipment—and a sharp decline in the quality of life. The following report from World War II gives a vivid sense of what it must have been like.

"For some time the harbour has been growing noisier at night and the heavy fogs of the last three weeks have increased this tendency. Last night was probably the worst since the war began. A convoy of fifty ships was crawling in all night, and in addition to the usual loud blowing for the medical boat, pilot launches, coal barges, navigation signals, etc., each vessel blew a fog warning every few yards. It was a still night, and to add to the din of customary shore fog whistles, buoys and bells, each of the ships anchored in the harbour—and there were dozens—maintained an anchor watch, who vigorously rang the ship's bell every minute or so. The whole thing was a bedlam which made sleep almost impossible....

Motorcycles, army and commercial trucks roar through the streets, dozens of locomotives shunt day and night with the usual bell-ringing and whistling, and last but not least the streetcars, now about eighty or ninety in number, pound over the dilapidated rails with a clatter that makes conversation almost impossible. At the same time, overhead there is the continuous monotonous droning of all kinds of planes. In fine weather they never let up even for one hour out of the twenty-four.

On the streets crowds throng the sidewalks until late in the night and every evening sees swarms of drunks reeling, singing or fighting on all the principal thoroughfares...."

[Report of H. B. Jefferson, July 29, 1943. Courtesy of the Public Archives of Nova Scotia.]

provided barracks for Canadian artillery and infantry units (along with German prisoners of war in the First World War). There were some stronger martial echoes when the old Magazines were used to store modern ammunition and when, in World War II, the fort became the centre for Halifax's anti-aircraft operations.

In 1951 the old fort's military function finally came to an end when it was handed over to the Canadian Parks Services, which began a multimillion dollar restoration project—still to be completed.

Even though it was a formidable fort for its day, it may be that the usefulness of the Citadel was never really the main idea. Colonel Nicholls had argued, "the good effect that the building of the fort would have on the Morale of the natives" was an excellent reason for its construction. He went on to say that potential enemies visiting Halifax, who "... see its shore bristling with cannon on every side, and the British flag flying on the Citadel, on a fort respectable and strong for this side of the Atlantic, are thoroughly deterred from making an attack on Halifax."

The fort was never to fire a shot in anger. It is perhaps in this that its success is most clearly reflected: as a monumental symbol of the imperial British Lion's resolve to defend its own against all comers.

START TOUR

Start and end point: Citadel Hill.
On foot: From the downtown area, Citadel Hill may be reached via the stairway at the head of George Street.
By car: Citadel Hill may be reached through the northwest and southeast entrances.
Time: One to two hours.

Old Town Clock

For almost two centuries the clock has been the city's best-known and most-loved landmark. Completed in 1803, it is the only building on Citadel Hill that is directly associated with Prince Edward, the Duke of Kent.

Planned by the Duke as a clock for his troops, it became a joint project of the army, navy, and town. With its octagonal three-tiered turret placed firmly on its rectangular base, the building shows a brisk and almost whimsical array of forms, from the Doric colonnade on the lowest level to the flared dome and ornamental ball on the top. Its blue clockface and gold numerals, ivory woodwork, Georgian doors, and curved staircases make the building an elegant survivor of the age.

The clock mechanism, made by the Royal clockmakers, has worked for almost two centuries—ticking steadfastly through the Great Explosion of 1917. The three bells hung in the open belfry continue to toll the quarter-hour, half-hour, and hour.

The rectangular building was first used as barracks for an overflow of men from the crowded fort. (It may have been during this period that an army deserter hid in the clock weights shaft before making his escape.) In 1829 it became the spacious accommodations of the "keeper of government clocks," who was paid £26 per annum; the clock-keeper position was supported until the British departure in 1906.

At the foot of Citadel Hill, below the Old Town Clock, is **Brunswick Street.** Formerly known as Barrack Street (it ran between two barracks below the north and south ends of the hill), for much of its history it was lined with a ramshackle array of rum shops, taverns, and bawdy-houses. They had vivid names, including Royal Oak, Daring Brig, Emerald Hall, and Black Dog, named for the canine who helped to maintain order. Frequented by garrison troops and by tars from the warships in the harbour, the street gained its informal name of "Knock-'Em-Down Street" from their frequently ungentle encounters.

By the 1870s, the town had had enough of the disorder and the drunkenness. (One citizen complained at the time that there was "Rum on the right hand and rum on the left; rum before you, rum behind you, and rum all around you!") The military authorities placed the street out of bounds to the troops, the city fathers proclaimed it "South Brunswick Street," and within a few years respectable brick buildings had arisen over the slums. These included the Salvation Army Citadel (built on the site of a particularly notorious tavern), the Visiting Dispensary, and the Halifax Academy; these three red brick buildings may be seen (left to right, respectively) along Brunswick Street to the south of the Old Town Clock.

···· *Before you enter the fort, glance back towards the harbour from the promontory near the main gate.*

Following in a long line of the Empire's warriors, Winston Churchill surveyed the scene from this point in the fall of 1943. Then, warplanes droned overhead, fighting men crowded the streets, and the harbour was filled with British and Canadian warships and the merchant vessels destined for the North Atlantic convoy run—all under his overall command (see box on page 156).

The Citadel

Summer: May 15 to June 14. Open 9:00 A.M.–5:00 P.M. June 15 to August 31. Open 9:00 A.M.–6:00 P.M. Small admission charge. Fort, authentic military displays from the 1870s, including sentry changes, drill, and the firing of the Noon Gun. Static displays, "Tides of History" audio-visual presentation; Army Museum, Citadel gift shop, refreshments. Parks Canada offers excellent guided tours.

Off-season: September 1 to October 15. Open 9:00 A.M.–5:00 P.M. Free admission. Noonday Gun and grounds open.

Call (902)426-5080 for further information.

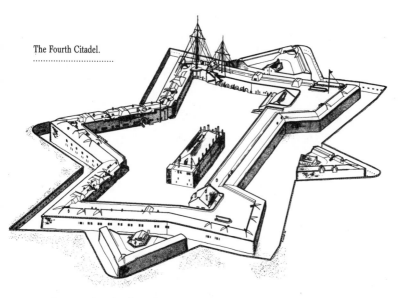

The Fourth Citadel.

···· *On entering the fort, directly in front of you is the Parade Square.*

The Parade Square was used for over a century by British and Canadian troops for parades and drills. Underneath it were

The Citadel

A Parade Square
B Cavalier Building
C Redan
D Southeast Salient
E South Ravelin
F Southwest Demi-bastion
G Curtain Wall
H West Ravelin
I Counterscarp Wall
J South Magazine

K Sally Port
L Ditch
M North Ravelin
N Northeast Salient
O Northwest Demi-bastion

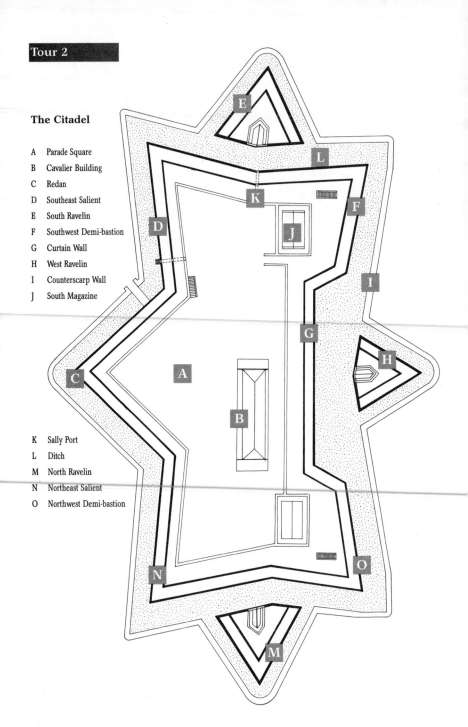

located three capacious water tanks; designed to collect rain water, they were intended to supply the garrison and possibly many townspeople during a siege.

···· *Across the Parade Square is the Cavalier Building.*

The Cavalier Building

Constructed between 1830 and 1832, this building consists of a series of robust ironstone casemates (vaulted rooms) that originally supported a heavy earth and stone roof (covered in 1855 by a timber roof) for a gun battery, and provided "bomb-proof" rooms for barracks and storage. Six cells for defaulters were located at the north end of the building.

When the fort was armed in 1854, seven 32-pounder cannon and their traversing platforms were mounted on the roof's west side. These weapons remained in place until the 1880s, but as early as 1855 the commanding officer wondered whether these heavy weapons "would not shake the walls very considerably and possibly bring them down." Fortunately, the building was never put to this test.

The **Cavalier Building** currently houses the Orientation Centre, the Army Museum, and a gift shop and refreshment centre. In the ground floor casemates are examples of the spartan barracks of nineteenth-century garrison troops.

···· *To your left as you enter through the main gate is a stone staircase. Take this to the ramparts and turn left at the top of the stairs.*

The Ramparts

At this point you are on the **Redan** ramparts. They are constructed largely of sod—rather than granite or ironstone—to reduce injuries to defending troops from flying fragments caused by enemy gunfire.

From the Redan ramparts there is an immediate sense of the fort's commanding position. (The view must have been far more striking when, as in the town's first century, few buildings in the town exceeded two or three stories in height.) Many stirring sights have been seen from the hill: In 1758, to take one example, 160 warships of the Royal Navy spread their sails across the harbour as they set out for the conquest of Louisbourg; a year later, they again set sail from here on Wolfe's expedition to Quebec.

Proceeding onward to the point of the Redan you pass two 7-inch rifled muzzle-loaders of the type mounted on the Redan from the 1870s, when the fort's role became that of a supporting sea battery. Looking out through the gun embrasure at the Redan's point towards the MacDonald Bridge, you can glimpse the naval dockyard in its time-honoured location. The role of the fort's guns in its defence can be easily envisioned.

Reversing direction and walking towards the signal masts on the **Southeast Salient,** you pass the 12-pounder gun used for the firing of the Noon Signal.

Looking in a southeasterly direction through the gun embrasure to the left of the masts, the small hump of Georges Island can be seen nearby. For many years, Fort Charlotte on the island, Fort Clarence on the Eastern Shore (where the oil tank farm is now), and the Grand Battery (where the Halifax Hilton is now) together formed the inner line of the harbour defences.

The **signal masts** were used to communicate vital shipping information. The taller mast (117 ft.) signalled the arrival in the harbour of commercial vessels: using a combination of company flags, discs, and pennants, it communicated the nationality, ownership and type of ship to the public.

The shorter mast (78 ft.) was used by the military to communicate to and receive information from the forts and signal stations further south toward the harbour approaches, including York Redoubt and stations at Camperdown and Sambro Island. A combination of balls, flags, and lanterns (at night) transmitted messages based on a secret numeric code. (See the Signals Display in the casemate below the masts.) From the embrasure next to the Signals Post there is a direct view south to Point Pleasant and York Redoubt.

Continuing west along the rampart towards the flagstaff, you can see the **South Ravelin,** the **ditch,** and the **glacis**—the slopes surrounding the fort, carefully sculpted and smoothed so as to afford no cover to attacking troops.

The flagstaff is on the **Southwest Demi-bastion,** one of the fort's strongest points. (The guns are the famous 32-pounder smooth-bore, a mainstay of the fortress's—and the Empire's—defences for much of the nineteenth century.) Through the embrasure the view is towards the west, the direction from which it was expected any major attack against the Citadel would come. **Camp Hill** can be seen about 650 m (600 yd.) away beyond the group of trees, identified by the tall chimneys of the

Camp Hill Hospital. This gentle knoll was a major worry to British military planners: if captured, enemy artillery mounted on it would pose a significant threat to the fort.

As you walk away from the flagstaff towards the Cavalier Building, the **Curtain Wall** offers a clear view of the **West Ravelin,** as well as the large ditch and the loopholes of the musketry gallery in the **Counterscarp Wall.**

Return to the parade ground level via the ramp next to the South Magazine; the ramp was used for hauling cannon and ammunition up to the ramparts.

South Magazine

To your immediate right as you return to the parade ground level is the South Magazine, one of two used to store the fort's gunpowder. It is powerfully built with 8 ft. thick walls and a heavy vaulted roof to deflect cannon fire.

Entering through one of the doors at either end of the building, note that the door handles, bolts, nails, and such are of copper or brass—rather than iron or steel—to prevent any accidental sparks; for the same reason, the floors were repeatedly swept and watered down. Smoking was prohibited in and around the building, and special slippers were worn by men working inside, to prevent sparks caused by hobnail boots.

The magazine's capacity was about two thousand barrels, each of which contained 90 lbs. of black powder. In addition to the powder stored here, there were small "expense" Magazines near the guns for immediate use. To keep the powder dry a special system of ventilation was installed, consisting of eight air shafts, copper-covered oak doors, and copper-shuttered windows.

On leaving the magazine you might like to take a closer look at the outer defences of the fort (below), or visit some of the exhibits and presentations in the different casemates.
- The "Tides of History" audio-visual show may be seen in the casemate beyond the ramp to your left.
- The Army Museum is located on the second floor of the Cavalier Building.
- The Citadels Exhibit—a display of models of the second, third, and fourth (current) Citadels is in the casemate under the stone staircase on the opposite side of the parade ground.
- The Signals Exhibit is located in the casemates directly under the signal masts.

···· *To reach the outer defences, as you leave the magazine proceed a few metres with the wall on your right and enter the sally port.*

The Outer Defences

The **sally port** gave troops everyday access to the outer defence works but would also be used to rush infantry into the ditch if needed to confront an enemy there.

As you leave the sally port and enter the **ditch,** there is an immediate sense of the forbidding strength of the fort, and how daunting to an enemy its conquest must have been. Nowhere in the ditch would an enemy be safe from the devastating fire that would rake it from the casemates and the musketry gallery. The casemates—two casemate openings—can be seen to your right—each held one 24-pounder cannon that would have been loaded with case shot or grapeshot.

To the left, in the **outer (or counterscarp) wall** can be seen the loopholes of the musketry gallery. This gallery extends around the entire fort, to be used by infantry to fire into the ditch. From the musketry gallery countermine tunnels were dug outwards under the glacis; these would have been used to destroy any tunnels being dug towards the fort by the enemy.

···· *Note: the sally port next to the Models Exhibition casemate in the Southeast Salient gives direct access to an entrance to the musketry gallery; you could also follow the ditch along the Southeast Salient to reach this entrance.*

Directly opposite the sally port exit is a set of wooden stairs giving access to the **South Ravelin.** This is one of three ravelins located in the Citadel's ditch, the others are outside the west and north walls. Completed in the 1840s, these triangular defence works were designed to provide overlapping fire onto the glacis and flanking fire into the ditch. They were originally armed with seven 32-pounder cannon, six firing through embrasures and one firing *en barbette* ("over the parapet").

The ravelin has extremely thick granite walls and was self-contained, with a strong double-storey guardhouse to provide cover for the defenders. The guardhouse was, in turn, provided with its own ditch to give added protection if the ravelin itself was overrun by invading troops.

···· *Return to the interior of the Citadel via the sally port.*

Point Pleasant Park

Tour 3 follows the line of the old forts and sea batteries. These all once commanded excellent vantage points towards the harbour channel and across the Northwest Arm. Today the inland ones are largely surrounded by trees, but the shoreline forts still afford fine views. Note that, with the exception of the Prince of Wales Tower, the forts are in varying stages of ruin and care should be taken when exploring them.

From the city's beginning, Point Pleasant has been its most popular recreation area. The park offers enchanting woodland and seashore walks with panoramic views of the Northwest Arm, the harbour channel, and McNabs Island, and is an ideal place for hiking or picnicking, or for watching vessels entering the harbour and the Arm.

For many years the most heavily fortified point in the harbour defences, the park is studded with old forts and sea batteries. Among them is the eighteenth-century Prince of Wales Tower, which has been impeccably restored and is well worth a visit, while the other defence works are easily accessible and offer imposing vistas.

Point Pleasant, Halifax Harbour (Englehart, 1860).

Introduction

Note: Tour 3 begins on page 95.

Around 500 million years ago, the slaty bedrock on which the city is built was laid down as deep-sea muds. Compressed, crushed, and folded, it was finally gouged by glaciers into the shape we see today—a peninsula with Point Pleasant at its southernmost tip, bounded by the Northwest Arm and the harbour. The park offers many examples of these geological processes.

When the British arrived in 1749 they were impressed by the point's strong position at the harbour entrance and set to work to build the town there. Within a few days, however, wiser counsel prevailed: seeing that the point was very exposed to southeasterly gales and that there were shoals offshore, which would hamper shipping, a new site further north was chosen.

Guarding the infant town against Indian attack became the main British concern, and, ironically, Point Pleasant was the chief worry. Well to the south, this untamed woodland was frequented by Micmac and only the well-armed or the foolhardy ventured there. In 1757 a party of strolling seamen was attacked; two were scalped and two were carried off into the forest. In the same year Cope, a Micmac chief who had fought against the British, disappeared, and tradition has it that he was killed in a fight and secretly buried somewhere on the point.

Once the Micmac had made peace, the townspeople made avid use of the point. People strolled or rode out from the town as a favourite recreation, while officers of the fleet and garrison cantered their mounts along the numerous bridle paths, a lovely and bracing alternative to a gallop on the Common.

Now, too, the British could include Point Pleasant in the town's defence: like the prow of a man o'war jutting towards the sea, its natural strength had stirred the British who saw that fortifications built here would prevent the passage of enemy ships into the inner harbour and up the Northwest Arm.

So, for almost two centuries the heavily fortified peninsula was a strongpoint in Halifax's defence. The first emplacements were built here in 1762, when the authorities, fearing a French attack, constructed two small works where the Point Pleasant and Northwest Arm Batteries were later built. Between 1779 and 1793 a number of small batteries sprang up around the point to defend against possible American and, later, French attacks;

*F*rom their winter hunting grounds inland—where caribou and beaver were plentiful and there was shelter from the fierce Atlantic storms—each spring the Micmac travelled to the forested wilderness of Chebucto harbour, where Halifax was later founded. They came by the lakes and portages or by sea in sturdy birch bark canoes so seaworthy that Micmac voyages to Newfoundland were not unknown.

They had lived in these parts for about two thousand years before the white man arrived and knew the harbour well. In the spring migratory birds flew in from the South; game and fish were plentiful. Where the city now stands, they trapped mink, caught trout from streams running down the hill, and hunted moose and wild duck in the marshy pools of what was to become the Common. Sea fish were abundant, and when enough game, fish, and fowl were brought in, they feasted and celebrated in the forest, on the

shores of the lovely Point Pleasant, and along the waters of the Northwest Arm. When in the 1500s the first Europeans arrived off Nova Scotia, their ships seemed to the Micmac to be islands covered with trees in whose branches bears clambered—but these were the palefaces that legend taught would come to rule them and take their land. By the end of the eighteenth century the Micmac, along with their French allies, had been defeated. The Micmac made peace, burying the hatchet in the Governor's garden on Spring Garden Road, and the long summer days of hunting, fishing, and celebration were at an end.

among these was Fort Ogilvie, which played a valuable role in the fortress until the end of the Second World War. In 1794 Prince Edward built a central keep to support the other batteries, naming it the Prince of Wales Tower.

In the 1860s, after the advent of rifled guns and amid fears of a new conflict with the Americans, the Point Pleasant batteries in cooperation with those on McNabs Island became the fortress's main line of defence. At the same time Cambridge Battery was built and armed with the new weapons, while Fort Ogilvie was reconstructed and rearmed. These two powerful works had a greater command of the sea around the point than the older batteries, which fell into disuse; the Prince of Wales Tower continued in use as an armed magazine.

By the beginning of the twentieth century, newer and more powerful weapons had shifted the main defence line further seawards, and Point Pleasant became part of the inner defence line. Fort Ogilvie and Cambridge Battery were rebuilt and armed with breech-loading guns, while Point Pleasant Battery was revived and armed with the new quick-firing guns. However, during the First World War only Fort Ogilvie and Point Pleasant Battery were active, and by the Second World War only Fort Ogilvie was used—as a training and reserve battery.

The point is also strongly associated with the city's greatest son, Joseph Howe. Born in 1804 in a small cottage on the Northwest Arm just outside the current park, his great love for his native land may have stemmed from his affection for this area, which he called "the enchanted ground." In later years, he practised his speeches in the quiet of the woods and was once called to fight a famous pistol duel on the ground next to the Prince of Wales Tower.

Today, thanks to the military's long use of the land, Point Pleasant is preserved as a park. For over a century the Crown kept intact almost 200 acres of choice property and in 1866 offered to lease it to the city for 999 years at an annual rent of one shilling—subject to the military's continued use in time of need. Seven years later the military cleared woods and laid out drives, and the Tower Woods became Point Pleasant Park. In early July each year the Point Pleasant Park Commission, consisting of nine citizens including the Mayor of Halifax, meets the Queen's Representative at the Prince of Wales Tower to present the annual rent.

Start and end point: Tower Road parking area in the park.
By car: From the downtown area, take Sackville Street to South
Park Street. Turn left onto South Park Street (which changes to
Young Avenue) and continue south. When you reach the park,
turn right on Point Pleasant Drive and continue one block to the
Tower Road parking lot, on your left.
By bus: From the downtown area, take the number 9 from Scotia
Square to the park's Tower Road parking lot.
Time: One and a half to three hours.

···· *From the parking lot, walk down Cambridge Drive to the Prince of
Wales Martello Tower (ten- to twelve-minute walk).*

Prince of Wales Tower

*Open July 1 to Labour Day, 10:00 A.M.–6:00 P.M. Free admission.
Call (902)426-5080 for further information.*

The **Prince of Wales Tower** is a pioneer work. Completed in
1798, it is the oldest of its kind in the world—and was the first of
five to be built in Halifax, of sixteen to be built in Canada, and of
dozens erected around the British seacoast during the Napoleonic
Wars.

Prince of Wales Martello Tower (Rutherford, 1877).

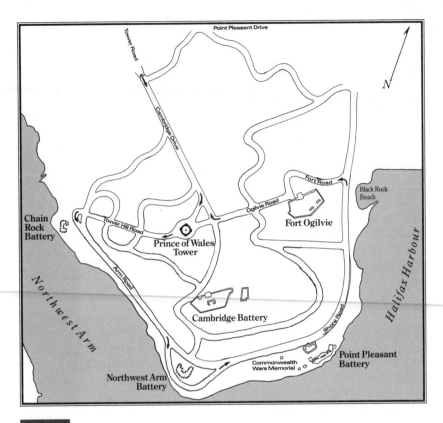

Tour 3

Point
Pleasant Park

In 1794 Prince Edward, the Duke of Kent, took over as
Commander-in-Chief in Halifax and almost immediately became
concerned about the defences on Point Pleasant. Although the
existing works were good sea batteries, they were very vulnerable to a land attack. Following the advice of his Commanding
Royal Engineer Captain James Straton, he decided that a central
fort be constructed on high ground. As the Prince described it,
the fort would be "in a situation not only most amply commanding the three Sea Batteries ... but also calculated greatly to annoy
an enemy that might attempt to land in the Northwest Arm."

The Prince and his Royal Engineer were almost certainly
inspired in their choice of design by the Cape Mortella exchange
during the French Revolutionary War, when heavy bombardment
by two British warships with 106 guns between them failed to
subdue a Corsican stone tower mounting just three smallish cannon. An affront of this magnitude to His Britannic Majesty's

Navy made its mark, and stone coastal defence "Martello" towers came to be thought of as nearly indestructible.

Edward was anxious to forge ahead with his tower. Apart from his passion for fort building, there was news of a French squadron in the western Atlantic. He began building it in the summer of 1796 and immediately ran head-on into the Board of Ordnance in London, which refused to fund the work, pointing out that prior approval was required before building any permanent structure. The Prince rejoined that the soil layer was so thin that he had no alternative but to build in stone—and then there was that French squadron. With additional pressure from the Prince's ally, the Duke of Portland, the Board relented and the tower was completed two years later. The Prince named it after his eldest brother George, the Prince of Wales.

The tower is a very strong structure, with ironstone walls 8 ft. thick at the bottom and 6 ft. thick at the parapet. When completed it had a parapet with twelve gun embrasures, giving it a crenellated and highly medieval appearance. About 1810 it was modified after the roof collapsed under the weight of the heavy carronades mounted on it.

In 1862, after the advent of rifled weapons made it vulnerable as a fort, the tower was remodelled as a central magazine for the other batteries, including the construction of four machicolated galleries (structures projecting outwards from the roof and allowing downwards and flanking musketry fire) on the roof; it was armed with 64-pounder rifled muzzle-loaders. This was the final version of the tower, still standing today.

By the end of the nineteenth century, the tower was very vulnerable to modern gunfire; its use, even in a secondary role as a magazine, was no longer realistic, and in 1881 the guns were removed.

Ground floor: As you enter the tower, the entranceway to the left leads to the magazine. Barrels of gunpowder stored here were for immediate use in the defence of the tower (the "Expense Magazine") and for the use of the other Point Pleasant batteries.

When built in 1798, this floor was intended as barrack space for forty-six officers, non-commissioned officers, and men, and there were musketry loopholes in the walls giving some light and ventilation. In fact, plans for manning the tower during a crisis were optimistic: if Halifax were attacked, seamen off merchant and other ships "that may chance to be in harbour" were to man

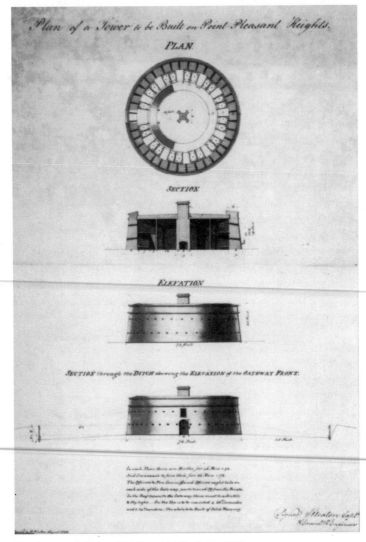

Plan of a tower to be built on Point Pleasant heights (Straton, 1796).

the tower, assisted by Volunteer Artillery, a few Royal Artillery, and some inhabitants of the town—who might, presumably, have been redirected from a pleasant stroll on the point.

The central pillar was equipped with powder hoists to lift the powder to the guns on the roof; it was originally a central stairway for passage from one floor to another.

HOWE'S DUEL

*O*n a chilly morning in March 1840, Joseph Howe, Nova Scotia's greatest politician, fought a duel on the open space next to the Prince of Wales Tower. He had been called out by a political opponent, John Halliburton, who had objected to one of Howe's editorials in the *Novascotian* criticizing his father, the Chief Justice.

Taking a chivalrous gamble, Howe stood his ground, his pistol lowered, and allowed his younger opponent a clear and unhurried shot. Halliburton missed. Howe—a fine shot—then carefully and deliberately took aim, and after what must have seemed like an aeon to the quaking man, pointed his pistol into the air and fired off the shot. Howe handed the smoking weapon to his second with the remark, "Let the creature live!" and the two walked away through the woods to a delayed breakfast.

First floor: This space was used as barracks for one non-commissioned officer and nineteen men, as well as for a small arms store holding swords, pistols, muskets, and boarding-pikes for the defence of the tower. In 1798 it provided barrack space for forty-six officers, non-commissioned officers, and men; it was also a gun platform for four 6-pounder guns (firing through the large portholes) and included twelve musketry loopholes in the walls.

Roof: This was a gun platform for four 32-pounder guns firing *en barbette* (over the parapet) with four machicolated galleries. In 1798 four 68-pounder carronades and two 24-pounder cannon were mounted on the roof.

For more than a century Point Pleasant was cleared of trees and the tower's roof offered a panoramic view out to the harbour entrance, to the Northwest Arm, and across the harbour channel to McNabs Island; there was also a commanding view of the fortifications fanning out from the tower—Fort Ogilvie and the Point Pleasant, Cambridge, and Northwest Arm Batteries.

As you leave the tower, note the ironstone bedrock on which it and the city are built.

WILDLIFE ON POINT PLEASANT

*T*he glaciers that shaped the peninsula and the harbour islands left behind a rocky soil, which, much enriched over the years, now supports a rich and varied wildlife—over 120 tree and plant species, over 150 bird species, and a wide variety of animals, insects, and fish have been recorded on and around the point.

Trees: In the eighteenth century the point was entirely cleared of trees—to give the military unobstructed views—but today again hosts a typical Nova Scotian coastal forest. The trees are largely native softwoods: White and Red Spruce, and White and Red Pine. Some more exotic species have been introduced, including Scots Pine, Douglas Fir, Norway Spruce, Witchhazel, and Horsechestnut. There is also a scattering of hardwoods, mainly Red and Sugar Maple, Red Oak, White and Yellow Birch, and European Copper Beech.

Plants: The forest floor is home to a colourful variety of shade-loving ground plants. These include the Blue-beaded Lily, the false Lily-of-the-Valley, the Ragged Fringed Orchid, the Wild Sarsaparilla (for years a key ingredient of root beer), and Goldthread (used in earlier centuries for cough medicine) named for its deep yellow roots. Many other names of plants found on the point simply glow with colour:

···· *From the tower entrance turn left and take Tower Hill Road down to the Northwest Arm.*

The long inlet known as the **Northwest Arm** has for many years been popular with Haligonians and their visitors for yachting—the jetties of clubs and private homes are found on both sides—and for swimming and skating. For many years, too, it was a worry to the fortress's defenders as a "rear entrance" to the town. Just below the road is the site of the old **Chain Battery;** the remains of the battery's earthen walls may be seen in the edge of the curved hollow. Built in 1796 by the Duke of Kent as a blunted Redan mounting four guns, it was designed to protect the celandine, meadowsweet, and chokecherry, yellow rocket, adder's mouth, and coltsfoot, bulbous buttercup, Three-toothed Cinquefoil, and Mouse-ear Chickweed. Several species of fern can be seen, including Cinnamon and Bracken Ferns, along with dozens of species of mushrooms.

Birds: Woodpeckers, blue jays, Red-breasted Nuthatches, and chickadees are common, while Black-backed and Herring Gulls, sea ducks, and the occasional Osprey may be seen close to the shore. Many other species have been recorded, including petrels, fulmars, cormorants, terns, puffins, loons, hawks, falcons, plovers, thrushes, kingfishers, and hummingbirds. In the spring and fall, migratory birds—warblers, Red-eyed Vireos, and sometimes an owl—rest in the park.

Other animals can be seen on and around the point. Red squirrels are everywhere, short-tailed shrews and white-footed mice may be seen, and at least one hare has been spotted. Salamanders, frogs, and turtles can also be seen. Along the shoreline the keen explorer can find many species of invertebrates, including mussels, periwinkles, and starfish. Offshore, seals can sometimes be spotted watching observers with the same interest we show them, while in the sea around them swim a variety of native fish, including Atlantic herring, mackerel, halibut, spiny dogfish, mummi-chog, sea raven, and butterfish.

....

chain boom that was stretched across the Arm to prevent French ships from sailing up it to land troops for an attack on the town. The first chain boom had been erected in 1762 after the French capture of Newfoundland; at that time a sloop armed with eight 6- or 9-pounder cannon was anchored inside the boom.

The boom was anchored on **Chain Rock** below the battery. The ring-bolt fitting embedded in the rock is thought to date from the War of 1812, while the concrete blockhouse was associated with British cable communications to York Redoubt and the other forts on the western side of the Arm in the late nineteenth century. Note also the deep grooves and fine striations in the rock, marking the passage of glaciers.

···· From Chain Rock continue along Arm Road to Purcell's Landing.

From 1853, **Purcell's Landing** was used by the Purcell family to ferry people and merchandise from the peninsula to the cove that also bears the family's name, as travel by the land route was difficult and time consuming. While plying their trade, the family was often instrumental in rescuing drowning Haligonians. Near the landing was the Government Wharf, used primarily for the ferrying of troops and military supplies between the wharf and Purcell's Cove for further portage to the forts and signal stations. If York Redoubt on the opposite shore came under attack, the military expected to use Purcell's ferry to carry troops across to help in the fort's defence.

···· As you proceed along Arm Road, you will see the gazebo.

Behind the gazebo are the ruins of the **Northwest Arm Battery,** designed to stop the passage of enemy ships up the Arm. From the promontory in front, the sweeping view of the entrance to the Northwest Arm makes clear how commanding was the battery's position.

The first version of the battery was built about 1762, at a site closer to the shoreline, amid fears of a French attack. Rebuilt during the American Revolution, in 1805 it was moved to its current location to avoid the sea erosion, which had destroyed the previous batteries. In its final version, it mounted four 32-pounder and three 18-pounder cannon, making it a fairly strong battery for the time. After the introduction of rifled ordnance in the 1860s, the cannon were removed and the battery fell into disuse.

Note, just in front of the earthen walls, the granite marker inscribed with the broad arrow, W. D., 1875, and S. M. The broad arrow and the W. D. signalled that this was British War Department property; S. M. stands for Survey Marker.

···· Continue eastwards along Shore Road

The **Commonwealth Wars Memorial** is a monument to the thousands of Canadian seamen who gave their lives in both world wars and in the Korean War, fighting at the side of the mother country to keep the Atlantic sea lanes open. Spotlit at night, it is a moving and welcome landmark for ships entering the harbour.

This peaceful stretch of sea between the point and McNabs Island was, as the **main harbour channel,** a key point in the fortress's defences for 150 years. In the summer of 1762, amid fears of a French attack, Admiral Lord Colville moored his seventy-gun flagship *Northumberland* in these waters to support the newly constructed batteries on Point Pleasant. In the 1860s and 1870s—after the advent of rifled guns—it became the main line of the Halifax defences.

Past the memorial are the ruins of the **Point Pleasant Battery.** In 1762 the first defence work was built here to prevent the passage of enemy ships into the harbour, a role fulfilled by batteries in this location until the end of the First World War.

By 1861 the battery was heavily armed, with ten 32-pounder cannon (and one 12-pounder for signalling), but after the advent of rifled weaponry it was eclipsed by Fort Ogilvie and the Cambridge Battery. Too close to the waterline and therefore very vulnerable to naval plunging fire, its guns were removed.

Within twenty years, advancing technology had created a new role for the battery: it was reconstructed in the mid-1880s to protect the minefield to be laid in wartime between Point Pleasant and McNabs Island. Armed with two 12-pounder quick-firing guns to stop fast torpedo boats, it was also provided with powerful searchlights for nighttime target location. (The searchlights were located in the small structure to the south of the battery.) During the First World War the battery protected the minefield and a submarine net between the peninsula and Ives Point. After the war, the battery saw no further use.

···· *Further along Shore Road is Black Rock Beach.*

Black Rock Beach has been a favourite bathing area for many years. In 1809 the body of an executed pirate was hung from a gibbet here, as an example to others; this grisly lesson remained in place until the Governor's wife was startled by it on a ride through the park, whereupon it was removed.

···· *Continue past Black Rock Beach to Fort Road, on the left near the parking lot. Proceed up Fort Road to Fort Ogilvie.*

Fort Ogilvie, on high ground overlooking the harbour channel, was the most valuable defence work on Point Pleasant, in

HARBOUR CHANNEL

*T*he harbour channel between the point and McNabs Island has seen a remarkable historical pageant: For many hundreds of years Micmac came into Chebucto harbour in the summer, rowing in from the sea in their robust canoes; almost four hundred years ago the French explorer de Champlain sailed into the harbour; in 1745 came the first warfaring fleet in the form of D'Anville's battered ships, struggling past this point.

From 1749, townsfolk watched the Empire and its allies' vessels pass through these waters: The great Royal Navy

fleets setting their sails for the capture of Louisbourg and Quebec; in 1776 General Howe's defeated forces retreating from Boston; during the War of 1812, the captured United States frigate *Chesapeake* brought in by HMS *Shannon;* in the long peace of the nineteenth century the haughty battleships of the Empire, "glittering with the special white and brass éclat of the North American station"; in two world wars, the great merchant convoys setting out on their hazardous Atlantic voyage to face the fearsome U-boats prowling beyond the harbour approaches.

Here too, in a moment of rare poignancy, on the eve of war in 1939 King George VI and Queen Elizabeth waved farewell to hundreds of Haligonians from the *Empress of Britain* as the ship, escorted by British and Canadian warships, the white hull bathed by the setting sun, pointed its bow towards a darkening Europe.

....

use from 1793 until the end of the Second World War.

When war broke out between Great Britain and Revolutionary France in 1793, the Commander-in-Chief in Halifax, General Ogilvie, hastily reconstructed the Point Pleasant batteries. He also built a new fort to augment the cross-channel fire, and with gusty bravado, named the new work after himself. The original fort was a small crescent-shaped earthen battery, mounting six 24-pounder cannon, which were maintained for almost seventy years until, in 1861, the guns were replaced by 32-pounders.

The fort was the only work on Point Pleasant to survive the rifled gun revolution that occurred a few years later, coinciding with fears of an outbreak of hostilities with the United States during the American Civil War. It was, however, extensively rebuilt and enlarged and by 1870 was practically a new work, functioning as a pair with the Cambridge Battery. Designed as a four-faced lunette—a sort of detached bastion—the two principal faces covered Ives Point on McNabs Island and the main ship channel out to sea; they were armed with a powerful battery of five 9-inch and five 7-inch rifled muzzle-loaders.

A loopholed wall protected the fort from the rear, with the barracks located just to the left of the gate, and the large magazine centrally placed.

In the late 1890s, the fort was remodelled into its present form and armed with two 6-inch breech-loading guns; the gun in place today was mounted about 1901. The fort was used during the First World War, but by the next war it was functioning only as a training and reserve battery, the last working fort on Point Pleasant.

···· *Continue along Fort Road to Cambridge Drive.*

···· *To conclude the tour, turn right on Cambridge Drive and head toward the Tower Road parking area.*

···· *To view the Cambridge Battery—the last battery to be built on Point Pleasant—turn left on Cambridge Drive and continue for a few minutes until you see the battery on the left.*

Designed for the new rifled guns, the construction of **Cambridge Battery** was authorized in July 1862 and completed in December 1868; the process was accelerated by fears of a new

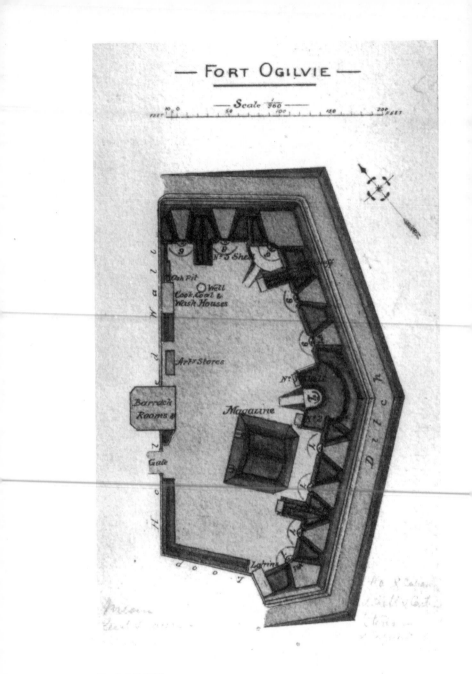

Fort Ogilvie (1877)

conflict with the Americans during the Civil War.

Named for the Duke of Cambridge, the professional head of the army through most of Victoria's reign, it was of similar design and coverage to Fort Ogilvie, the principal faces covering Ives Point on McNabs Island and the main ship channel. It worked in cooperation with Fort Ogilvie and was heavily armed with five 10-inch and three 7-inch rifled muzzle-loaders.

In the 1890s the battery was reconstructed for two 6-inch breech-loaders, leaving intact the old **RML Emplacements** in the right face. By the First World War the Point Pleasant defences had decreased in importance, and Cambridge Battery was no longer armed.

To the southwest of the battery are several beds of **purple heather,** said to have been sown by Scottish soldiers who had emptied their straw mattresses there.

···· *To complete the tour, return to the Tower Road parking area along Cambridge Drive.*

York Redoubt via the Northwest Arm

Tour 4 describes several sites of historic interest on the Northwest Arm en route to York Redoubt in addition to a tour of the fort.

The historic fort, set high on its granite bluff at the harbour entrance, played a vital role in the Halifax fortress from the eighteenth century to the 1950s. It offers commanding views across to McNabs Island and a splendid panorama of the Atlantic approaches—a perfect point for viewing ships entering and leaving the harbour. As well, the short drive to the fort affords fine views of the Northwest Arm.

Introduction

Note: Tour 4 begins on page 111.

Halifax from York Redoubt (from Picturesque Canada, 1882).

Over time, York Redoubt proved the most important of all the harbour defences. As early as 1699 the French had hoped to construct their main fort here. They saw clearly—as did the British a century later—that the bluff on which the fort now stands is a superb position for a sea battery: it is well situated to command the harbour mouth and has an imposing height that would keep it well out of reach of smooth-bore naval fire.

Adding to the position's natural strength, it was surrounded by tangled woods, which would have made an attack from the landward side very arduous; on the other hand, its relative vulnerability to naval landing parties was a major concern for much of its long history.

The development of the fort occurred in four stages:
- After the French Revolution, spurred on by Prince Edward.
- In the mid-1800s, after the introduction of rifled guns, involving two major reconstructions.
- At the beginning of World War II.

Defences Against the French

In 1793, after the French Revolution, the British in Halifax received reports of French warships in the western Atlantic. Fearing an attack, they hurriedly threw up defences around the town. One of these was a two-gun earthen battery on Sandwich Point (as the bluff was then known). Such a small work was incapable of inflicting any real damage on enemy ships trying to enter the harbour; rather, it was intended to harass and "soften them up" and to give advance warning of their presence.

Within a few years, Prince Edward, Duke of Kent, had commanded the expansion and strengthening of the battery. Eight 24-pounder cannon were mounted behind a crescent-shaped earthwork, protected against a land attack by palisades and a wooden blockhouse. In 1798 the blockhouse was replaced by a Martello Tower; in the same year, the Duke named the work York Redoubt in honour of his brother, the Duke of York.

But even this strengthened fort could not seriously impede enemy ships, as its cannon simply could not reach effectively across the harbour channel (see map on page 32). Yet it had become an important element in the harbour's defence system through the signal station on the tower, which could be used to communicate information on ship movements northwards to the Citadel and southwards to Camperdown.

Rifled Guns

For the next sixty years, nothing much happened at the redoubt except the maintenance recommended by the Duke of Wellington's 1825 commission (the same commission that recommended the construction of the current Citadel).

But in the 1860s the military community was jarred awake by

the advent of the rifled gun. Almost overnight, the defence system and its armaments—including York Redoubt with its smooth-bore cannon—were made obsolete. Adding to the general alarm, after the American Civil War there was anxiety about the intentions of the huge and victorious Union forces.

So, starting in 1863 the engineers expanded and completely remodelled the fort to accommodate the new rifled muzzle-loaders (or RMLs as they were known). The old eight-gun crescent battery was reconstructed as emplacements for three 10-inch RMLs, and the fort was extended southwards towards the hill, with new emplacements for eight 9-inch RMLs. Of the old work, only the tower survived.

This *First RML Reconstruction* continued until 1877, including a loopholed concrete Gorge Wall, built immediately to the rear of the guns as protection against overland attack, and a large new magazine, built, curiously enough, outside the wall. With the mounting of its powerful and far-ranging new weapons, York Redoubt had become a formidable first line in the harbour defences—at last worthy of its dominating position on the bluff.

As well, its strength was greatly enhanced by rifled guns in an indirect way. Although the fort's height above the sea gave powerful advantages, the guns could not cover the sea near the foot of the bluff; this meant that an enemy could land naval parties in the cove to attack the fort, unhampered by its guns. The possibility caused much uneasiness over the years—the erection in 1814 of Sherbrooke Tower, where the lighthouse on McNabs Island is now, was an attempt to deal with the problem, but it was not satisfactorily solved until the advent of rifled guns. These long-range weapons mounted on McNabs Island could easily reach the area below the bluff.

In 1888 a new spate of building occurred, known as the *Second RML Reconstruction*. The fort was further expanded to include the magazine and Position Hill (where the Fire Command Post was later built) within a new Gorge Wall. This greatly strengthened the fort's situation—Position Hill overlooked the fort, and its capture by an enemy would have been disastrous. Further strengthening the fort was the inclusion in the wall line of a Caponier—a work designed to provide flanking fire along the fort's walls—with two 64-pounder guns for landward defence.

Hardly had this reconstruction been completed than it was realized that the fort had, once again, been made obsolete by new technology. The newly mounted RMLs were powerful but were not comparable to the even newer breech-loading guns (or BLs), which were loaded from the rear of the barrel rather than from the muzzle. The BLs' greater range and hitting power meant that enemy ships armed with them had to be stopped even further out in the harbour approaches. York Redoubt was no longer an ideal location, so Sandwich Battery was built to the south. The old redoubt was soon eclipsed, and by 1906—when the British left Halifax—it had no role in the fortress.

For three decades the fort lay idle. During the First World War it was, however, used for barracks for the infantry guarding the newer forts in the area and, later, to house the overflow from Halifax of troops going to the Western Front.

Second World War

As war clouds gathered in the late 1930s, defence planners decided that York Redoubt was an excellent location for the Fire Command Post, which would coordinate the harbour defences. A new concrete structure—most of it underground—was built on Position Hill to contain range-finding and radio communications equipment. From relative obscurity, the old fort had become the nerve centre of the harbour defences.

In addition, an antisubmarine net was strung from Sleepy Cove below the fort to Mauger Beach on McNabs Island. To protect the net, the authorities built York Shore Battery, which included two gun emplacements, director towers, and searchlights.

After the war, York Redoubt was the only fort still garrisoned at the harbour entrance. Finally, in 1956 the fort was disarmed along with the other coastal defences, and York Redoubt's long and distinguished role in the defence of Halifax and the Empire came to an end.

....
START TOUR

Start point: Armdale Rotary.
End point: York Redoubt.
By car: From the downtown area, take Sackville Street and Bell Road to Quinpool Road; at the Armdale Rotary take Purcell's Cove Road (Route 253); a fifteen-minute drive.
By bus: Take number 1 bus to Sears and transfer to number 15.
Time: One and a half to three hours.

Northwest Arm

This ocean inlet separates the Halifax peninsula from the Nova Scotia mainland. Like the other waters around the town, it was once rich with fish: cod, herring, mackerel, lobster, rockfish, flatfish, eel, mussels, and other species abounded here.

The Micmac held their springtime celebrations near the head of the Arm, and used a word for it that the English heard as Waegwoltic, "the feast." By 1784, the English had established as many as twelve fisheries along the Arm to exploit the lavish stocks. In later years the Arm has been called "the valley of the giants" from the number of Premiers and other great figures born here; Joseph Howe was one, born on the Arm, in a house just north of the current Point Pleasant Park.

Shortly after turning onto **Purcell's Cove Road** (Route 253), you will see Spinnaker Drive on your left. A short way along it, at the junction of Anchor Drive, is a small **monument to the Great Explosion of 1917.** Mounted on a plinth is the anchor shank of the ammunition ship *Mont Blanc,* which blew up after a collision in the harbour narrows, devastating the city. The shank, weighing over half a ton, landed here after being tossed well over two miles—one of only two recognizable pieces of the ship found after the explosion.

A few hundred metres further along Purcell's Cove Road, **Melville Cove** appears on your left. Melville Island was originally used by fishermen until 1804, when the Crown paid £1,000 for the island and named it for Viscount Melville, the First Lord of the Admiralty.

The British used the island for a prison, as it was easily secured. Several wooden barracks were constructed to house captured French seamen; during the Napoleonic Wars, Haligonians travelled out to the prison on Sundays to purchase small models of ships made by French prisoners from beef bones. These prisoners were to be followed in a long procession by captured American seamen, escaped American slaves, Joseph Howe's Irish-American recruits for the Civil War, British military offenders, and bringing up the rear, German World War I prisoners of war.

The main prison buildings were destroyed by fire in 1936, leaving the chapel and officers' quarters; these—the nearest whitewashed and ironstone buildings—may be glimpsed from Purcell's Cove Road. The island is currently occupied by the Armdale Yacht Club.

ESCAPED

From the Naval Prison on Melville Island on the night of 28th April—PIERRK TRANK, a French Prisoner of War; about six feet high; fair complexion; dark eyes, and long black hair; speaks good English; and is the man who formerly lived as a servant to Sir John Wentworth.

The usual reward of ONE GUINEA will be paid for his apprehension, as also any reasonable expences which may be occurred. Said Trank has been seen on Windsor Road.

JOHN MACKELLAR
Agent for Prisoners of War.
(From the *Nova Scotian Royal Gazette*, November 28, 1809.)

Barracks of the Foreign Legion, Melville Island (Band, 1855).

···· As you continue up the hill a few hundred metres, on the left is the entrance to Fleming Park, a good spot from which to view the Arm.

Fleming Park was donated to the city by Sir Sandford Fleming (1827-1915), known to Canadians as the chief engineer in the construction of the Canadian Pacific Railway, completed in 1880. He was also a pioneer in world communications, inventing the concept of Standard Time. In 1897 he was knighted for his accomplishments.

Sir Sandford handed over the park on condition that the city build on it a tower. The **Dingle Tower** was erected in 1908 to commemorate the anniversary of the granting of representative government to Nova Scotia in 1758, the first such government in the British Empire. Dominions and colonies across the Empire, British cities, and Canadian provinces and universities contributed panels of native stone. The lower portion of the tower is rough-hewn as a remembrance of pioneer days, while the finely cut upper section is supposed to reflect more comfortable recent history. Flanking the entrance are replicas of the imperial lions that guard Nelson's column in Trafalgar Square.

···· Return to Purcell's Cove Road and continue along it, past Purcell's Cove, until you see signs for York Redoubt, the turn-off to which is on the left.

York Redoubt

June 15 to Labour Day: 10:00 A.M.–6:00 P.M, daily. Entry to World War II Fire Command Post; static display of history of the fort. Free admission.

Off-season: Park grounds open 9:00 A.M.–5:00 P.M. Free admission. Call (902)426-5080 for further information.

···· From the parking lot, head away from the hill towards the harbour channel.

The first structure, incorporated as part of the wall on your right, is the remaining first storey of the Martello tower, built in 1799. Originally armed with six guns on its wooden upper storey, its greatest use was as a signal station. The guns were removed in 1856, and the upper storey was gutted by fire in the 1890s.

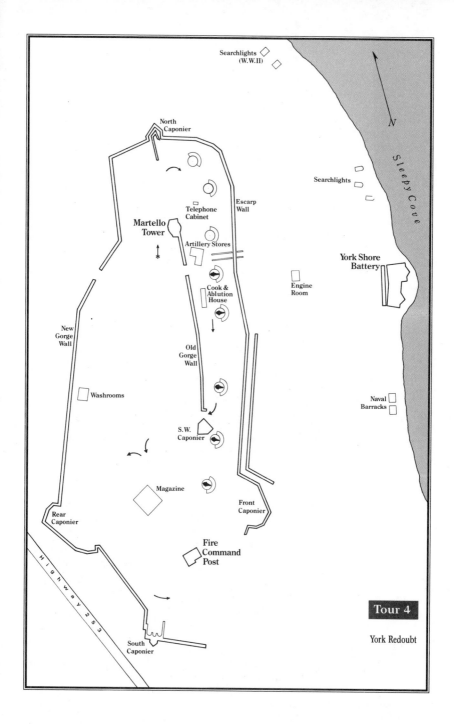

Searchlights
(W.W.II)

North
Caponier

Searchlights

Escarp
Wall

Telephone
Cabinet

Martello
Tower

Sleepy Cove

N

Artillery Stores

York Shore
Battery

Cook &
Ablution
House

Engine
Room

Old
Gorge
Wall

New
Gorge
Wall

Washrooms

Naval
Barracks

S.W.
Caponier

Rear
Caponier

Magazine

Front
Caponier

Fire
Command
Post

Tour 4

Highway 253

York Redoubt

South
Caponier

The Battle of the Atlantic

"*T*he only thing that ever really frightened me during the war," wrote Winston Churchill, "was the U-boat peril." In her struggle with Hitler's Germany, Britain's very survival depended on keeping the sea routes safe from attacks by German submarines. Without the ships bringing food, arms, and men across the Atlantic, she faced certain defeat.

During the early dark years of the war, Halifax was probably "the most important port in the world," as a British Rear Admiral put it. The anchor of the North Atlantic lifeline, it was also the main base for the naval and air forces which protected it. Huge shipping convoys assembled in Bedford Basin to be escorted across the Atlantic by the British Royal Navy and the Royal Canadian Navy whose ships left from their base in the dockyard, while aircraft flew from Shearwater in a constant hunt for the deadly U-boats.

In September 1939 the first convoy left Halifax, consisting of eighteen ships escorted by HMCS *St. Laurent* and *Saguenay*. During the course of the war, over 17,500 ships crossed the ocean in convoy. The headquarters for the command and control of the convoys and for the battle against the U-boats was in a modest building on Barrington Street; on occasion, sounds of exploding depth-charges at the harbour approaches could be heard in the town.

The Atlantic voyage was grotesquely hazardous. Apart from the often appalling weather, by the end of the first year of the war the Germans had sunk 1,281 ships—almost a quarter of Britain's pre-war merchant fleet. Typical of those days was the experience of Convoy HX79, consisting of forty-nine ships, which sailed from Halifax in October 1940. The HX79 had a powerful escort, and there was some confidence for its safe crossing, but the U-boat wolf packs were waiting. In spite of frantic efforts by the British warships, twelve merchant ships were sunk, with two more badly damaged.

In 1942, another thousand ships were sunk by the U-boats, and the situation was desperate. But the tables turned. In this "war of groping and drowning, of ambuscade and stratagem, of science and seamanship" as Churchill put it, British, Canadian, and later, American naval and air forces gradually perfected their tactics and equipment—much helped by top-secret intelligence—while Canadian corvettes roamed the seas in ever-larger numbers and aircraft exacted an increasing toll. In May 1943, having suffered great losses, the U-boats were withdrawn from the North Atlantic.

The war, grinding on for another two years, saw much-improved U-boats return to the convoy routes. But the Battle of the Atlantic had been won—close as it was. Had the U-boats triumphed, Britain would have fallen, there would have been no base for the D-day invasion, and the history of the Second World War—and of our world—would have been immeasurably different.

....

.... *Continue towards the emplacements at the northernmost part of the fort.*

From this vantage point the natural strength of York Redoubt's location can be clearly seen, commanding as it does the harbour entrance between the bluff and McNabs Island. Until the introduction of rifled guns, the fort could not, however, prevent enemy ships from passing—the range of smooth-bore cannon was just too limited.

The two **gun emplacements** are on the approximate location of the original eighteenth-century crescent battery; log palisades extended from the tower to the battery, enclosing it on both sides. Later three 10-inch RMLs were mounted here on pivots, with wide arcs of fire to keep a ship under fire longer as it passed up the harbour; they also had the ability to prevent ships from anchoring in the harbour and bombarding the dockyard. The two current emplacements were built during the early twentieth century to mount quick-firing guns.

.... *Turn away from the sea and walk southwards, towards the hill.*

View of York Redoubt from Sleepy Cove near Halifax (Petley, 1837).

On your left is the **main line of emplacements,** built for the seaward RML guns. The weapons on view were mounted during the Second RML Reconstruction (1888) and are of two calibres: 9 inches (weighing 12 tons and firing a 256-pound shell) and 10 inches (weighing 18 tons, firing a 400-pound shell); their effective range was up to 6,000 yds. They had crews of nine and eleven men, respectively, who used a combination of pulleys, tackle, and davits to load the shells. Ammunition for immediate use was stored in Expense Magazines (currently buried to preserve them), located between the emplacements.

The **Old Gorge Wall** on the right was built during the First RML Reconstruction (1863) for landward defence, and originally included musketry loopholes. It is not particularly robust: the real concern was to fend off attacks from naval landing parties rather than from a full-fledged assault, and if attacked by a larger force, the wall would hopefully give the defenders enough time to destroy the guns and so prevent their being turned on the other forts and the town.

From the flagstaff position there is a fine view of the harbour approaches, and of the area of sea covered by the guns.

As you continue southwards, you will see the **Artillery Store** (built between 1870 and 1873), used to house various pieces of hardware for working the guns.

On the left, the **East Caponier Passage** led to an ironstone caponier (a small but strong building projecting beyond the wall of the fort), that flanked the fort's East Ditch. The caponier has been demolished, and the passage now provides access to the ditch and to the road leading to Sandy Cove and the York Shore Battery (for the tour of the York Shore Battery, see page 120–21).

The **Cook and Ablution House** (built about 1873) contained—all in the one building—the Cook House, Bread and Meat Store, Field Forge, Lamp Store, and Ablution House (where the garrison washed themselves). Currently the building houses a small display of military hardware.

At the end of the wall is the **Southwest Caponier,** which provided flanking fire for the Gorge Wall; it was the southern-most building in the fort at the end of the First RML Reconstruction period.

···· *Following the road, approach the magazine via the hollow on the left.*

The **magazine** was built outside the fort during the First RML Reconstruction—probably because the hollow where it is located made the construction of a below-ground building easier—but was connected to the fort by means of a loopholed log stockade. It consists of two brick arched vaults, covered by a thick concrete slab and a thick layer of earth. To keep the ammunition dry, it had a sophisticated ventilation system, which in 1898 was augmented by its own boiler house for heat.

Continuing along the road, on the right is the **New Gorge Wall,** built during the Second RML Reconstruction, which extended the fort to include Position Hill. As with the Martello Tower and the Old Gorge Wall, the new wall was designed to fend off smallish land attacks.

The **South Caponier** forms the southernmost work of the fort. Originally armed with two 64-pounder smooth-bore cannon, the caponier also provided flanking musketry defence along the ditches of the south wall.

···· *Continue on to Position Hill.*

From this point can be seen the harbour approaches out to the Atlantic Ocean, as well as Chebucto Head, where signal stations and observation posts were located. Several hundred metres to the southeast is a hill, on top of which was built Sandwich Battery; in the 1890s it superceded York Redoubt in importance.

The **Fire Command Post** was built at the beginning of the Second World War and was designed to coordinate harbour defences in the event of an enemy attack. It was built in two levels, with the underground section considerably larger.

The building visible above ground is a steel-shuttered observation room. It housed various instruments, including the Depression Position Finder (still in place) for computing the range and bearing of ships. Today the observation room also houses an intriguing collection of nineteenth-century photographs of York Redoubt and the surrounding forts.

The underground section was designed to be safe from the effects of bombs, shells, and poison gas. It contained radio and telephone equipment linked to harbour batteries and observation posts, as well as the Fortress Plotter, which combined information from the various observation posts to plot the course of ships. On the upper level is a temporary display on York Redoubt and the harbour defences.

*This completes the tour of York Redoubt. The following brief section offers a tour of **Sleepy Cove** and the **York Shore Battery**, constructed during the Second World War. Note that the battery is in a state of semi-ruin; care should be taken when exploring it. The walk involves some steep sections and takes approximately forty-five minutes.*

···· *Take the East Caponier Passage to the ditch of the fort, and turn right along the road.*

From the road, note the **Escarp Wall**'s ironstone construction—the same native material used in the building of the Citadel.

All the buildings towards the cove are of World War II construction. A few metres along the road is the **Engine Room,** which generated power for the guns and searchlights in the cove below. Turning along the cove road after the steep section of track, you will see the naval barracks on the right.

···· *Continue along the road to York Shore Battery.*

York Shore Battery guarded the antisubmarine net, which was stretched between the cove and McNabs Island as protection against German U-boats. It consists of two quick-firing gun emplacements (each emplacement mounted twinned guns), director towers, and, further along the shore, searchlights for illuminating targets for the guns.

···· *Follow the road back up the hill to return to York Redoubt.*

Next to the main entrance to the fort is a collection of the guns that armed Halifax during the eighteenth and nineteenth centuries: smooth-bore cannon, rifled muzzle-loaders, and one breech-loader. The 10-inch breech-loader is of particular interest: once mounted at Fort McNab on McNabs Island, it was the largest gun ever mounted at the Halifax fortress.

North End

Tour 5 covers points of interest in the old North End, including St. George's Church and other buildings of historic interest on Brunswick Street, the dockyard, Admiralty House, and Fort Needham Park (site of the Halifax Explosion memorial). For the zealous explorer, there are also descriptions of sights beyond the North End, including the Prince's Lodge rotunda and Hemlock Ravine, which offers delightful woodland walks.

Please note that the different sections of the complete tour may be best reached by car. While the Brunswick Street area is easily walkable from downtown, and Admiralty House and Fort Needham Park can be reached by the energetic walker or by bus, a car is required to enjoy the sights beyond the North End.

Halifax from Fort Needham (Hicks, 1801).

The North End is one of the city's most historically intriguing areas. The home of the oldest naval dockyard in North America, whose ships guarded imperial interests for two centuries, it also contains a number of important public and domestic buildings from the eighteenth and nineteenth centuries, including St. George's Church, the "Little Dutch Church," and Admiralty House.

It is the site of the Great Explosion of 1917—the greatest man-made explosion prior to the atomic bomb—which cost thousands of lives and devastated the area. Rebuilt from the ruins in the 1920s, the North End is today characterized by a vibrant sense of community along with its traditional naval and military presence.

Introduction

Note: Tour 5 begins on page 127.

In 1753 a small group of German immigrants arrived in the infant town to reinforce the first group of settlers. They settled on two lanes running north from Citadel Hill, naming them Brunswick and Gottingen Streets; a few years later they built a small church—the "Little Dutch Church"—which stands to this day.

In 1759 His Majesty's navy established the King's Yard on two acres of land on the waterfront, directly below the new German church. This was used for the supply and refitting of naval vessels and as the site of a hospital for contagious diseases, such as malaria and yellow fever. The Yard gradually expanded northwards, and as the Napoleonic Wars ended—as if to confirm its permanent presence—the navy built a mansion for its Admiral on the rise overlooking the dockyard.

The Yard needed protection from a land attack, most pressingly during the American War of Independence when an attack led by George Washington himself was feared and Nova Scotian loyalty to the Crown was in doubt. In 1776 the engineers raised wooden defences around the dockyard and built Fort Needham on a hill to the north to cover the landward approach.

This war also brought the first black settlers. Many of these refugees—Loyalists and the slaves of white Loyalists—ultimately settled on the northern outskirts of the town. This northward stream of humanity was to continue until well after the War of 1812.

From these beginnings the North End saw little change until the 1840s: the area to the west of Gottingen Street remained open fields, while a house built near North Street was so isolated it was known as the "North Pole." But, as trade and shipbuilding flourished in the so-called Bluenose Age, the town expanded northwards and became a prime residential location—large plots, grand views of the harbour, and the magnetic presence of Admiralty House all added a certain lustre.

In 1854 the large Wellington Barracks was built on Gottingen Street. After Confederation, the Intercolonial Railway was pushed

AFRICVILLE

*I*n a small park overlooking the Bedford Basin is a memorial to the community that once existed there. Every year people gather for a reunion at the spot to celebrate Africville and the force of its memory.

During Halifax's earliest, roughest years, people of African heritage arrived in waves: Black Loyalists and slaves escaped from their American masters in the wake of the American Revolution; fierce Maroons from Jamaica (having

Selling
Mayflowers
*(Canadian
Illustrated
News,* 1872).

laid down their arms after a 140-year battle against the British; and refugees from the United States after the War of 1812. Life in the garrison town was hard, and the new arrivals were met by indifference and often hostility. In spite of their exertions most remained in poverty, and within a few years many left in despair for Sierra Leone or Trinidad. Many, however, stayed on, determined to make a life in their new home.

Of all the black communities that began quietly to put down roots, Africville was unique. It had a fine location, commanding a magnificent view over the basin, its small houses clustered around the Baptist church that was its heartbeat. People picked blueberries on the hillside or sledded down it in winter, and swam or skated from the shore. They bore direct witness to some of history's panoramas as the great convoys of the world wars filled the basin; and the famous might drop by—residents mention visits from Joe Louis and Duke Ellington. Above all, there was community, and over time Africville took hold in people's affections. As one elderly resident put it: "It was lovely, lovely ... the most beautiful sight you could want to see, Africville."

It lacked, however, recognition from the Halifax city fathers. Africville's people, mostly poor and without political clout, carried little weight with the authorities, and their pleas for protection and improved services fell on deaf ears. Over time, industry encroached, including a stone-crushing plant and an abattoir. Finally, an open city dump was located nearby. Inevitably, conditions in Africville deteriorated. A community petition addressed to the authorities in 1919 describes "bootlegging and raucous living ... and an utter disregard for the Lord's Day," while black parents from other parts of town warned their youngsters to stay well away.

Without proper policing or services, Africville was in serious trouble. In the 1960s the city decided to demolish the homes and to move the residents to modern housing. For many in the community the move meant a real opportunity to better their situation, but others—particularly the older residents—wanted to stay. "Pa" Carvery, for one, was determined to hold out. In a desperate move (engineers were waiting to build the new MacKay bridge) the authorities showed him a suitcase of money which would be his if he left. He declined the offer but finally left in early 1970. Africville was razed, and a long chapter in Halifax's community life was closed.

Today Africville burns bright in people's memories. To the city's assured and dynamic black community—Canada's oldest—it remains a symbol of the frequent indifference of the dominant culture, but perhaps even more as a celebration of the richness of human spirit and community that was there.

along the shoreline to North Street, the Deep Water Terminals were built. Greatly helped by the new railway, industrial activity accelerated as the end of the century drew near. In the Richmond area, between Fort Needham and the harbour, the towering Halifax Sugar Refinery—at nine storeys the tallest building east of Montreal—the Nova Scotia Cotton Company, and a major milling plant all began operations, along with a variety of other vigorous industries, including the manufacture of railway cars, stoves, furnaces, and paint. Nestled close to the industrial smokestacks, the workingman's suburb of Richmond flourished.

Almost all of this was swept away by the Great Explosion of 1917. Many hundreds of people were killed and injured, the Richmond area was laid waste, and there was major destruction as far as North Street.

Although planning for the North End's reconstruction began within a few days of the explosion, the postwar depression slowed everything down and many people refused to move back, feeling the area was cursed. However, by 1921 the Hydrostone area near Fort Needham was completed. During the Second World War, when the city's swollen population spilled into the area, the old scars were covered and healed. (In 1945, in a grim reminder of the 1917 disaster, the North End was evacuated when the Bedford Magazine—on the opposite side of the harbour—blew up. This time no damage was done to the suburb.)

Since the end of the war, the North End has undergone major urban renewal. Along Brunswick Street, many of the old buildings have been razed and replaced by low-income housing, while some streets close to the Citadel have been gentrified. In the most difficult and controversial move, the black township of Africville—largely unscathed in the devastation of 1917—was razed, to be replaced by Seaview Park and the highway system for the new MacKay Bridge; the residents were moved to newer development projects in the North End.

Today, with the naval dockyard still in its hallowed location and with the naval and military facilities at Stadacona, Willow Park, and Windsor Park, the North End retains much of its old flavour. Spread among these is a patchwork of communities, which make the North End the most varied and vibrant area of the city.

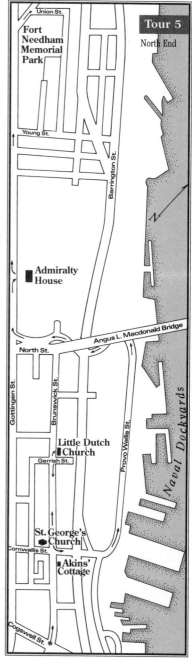

Start point: Brunswick Street, north of the Citadel.

End point: Downtown Halifax.

By car: Although Brunswick Street is easily reached on foot, a car is best for the tour.

By bus: To reach Admiralty House or Fort Needham Park, take the number 7 from Scotia Square.

Time: One to three hours.

···· *On Brunswick Street—the street directly below the Old Town Clock—proceed north past the intersection at Cogswell Street.*

On your left, just past Cogswell Street, is a group of twelve red brick houses, originally named the **Churchfield Barracks** (at 2046–68) and more recently known as the "Twelve Apostles." Built in 1901 in a familiar imperial style as quarters for married soldiers, they are among the few remaining examples of Victorian military dwellings in the city. Although they appear cramped and regimented, they were a vast improvement over the general living conditions of British troops in the nineteenth century, when marriage was heavy-handedly discouraged, and families usually had to make do in ordinary barracks, with nothing more than a blanket between them and the other soldiers.

On the same side of the street on the next block is the first of several houses on Brunswick Street associated with the West family; descended from Johann Wust, who arrived from Hesse Germany in 1751, the family became wealthy in West India shipping, trading fish for Caribbean rum, sugar, and molasses. The **parsonage** (at 2138) and **townhouses** (at 2140–46) were constructed in 1878 for the Universalist Church, of whom the Wests were major benefactors; in the 1860s and 1870s they built their own homes in the fashionable area along Brunswick Street.

On the other side of the street is **Akins' Cottage** (at 2151), the oldest private dwelling in Halifax. It was built in the 1790s on the outskirts of the rugged military town by a shipwright from the King's Yard, and in 1836 it became the home of Thomas Akins, Canada's first archivist and a tireless compiler of early Halifax records and anecdotes. (His work is, incidentally, a major source for this guide.) It is appropriate that his spare home, strongly reminiscent of British stone cottages of the day, should remain as the surviving example of early Halifax dwellings.

···· *On the northwest corner of Brunswick and Cornwallis Streets is St. George's Church.*

St. George's Church

St. George's Church, a National Historic Site, is North America's first round church. It basks in the distinction of having been initiated by a personal sum of £200 given by King George III to start construction—the only church known to have been conceived of by a member of the British Royal Family. (Another £500 was granted from the Arms Fund, money from the sale of weapons captured by the British in Maine during the War of 1812—one of several inadvertent New England contributions to the city's institutions.)

The King's interest in the church was fanned by his son, Edward, the Duke of Kent. Edward, perhaps because of his Hanoverian ancestry, had taken under his wing the local German congregation, who were outgrowing their small church further along Brunswick Street.

In 1800 Sir John Wentworth laid the foundation stone, and the church was completed in 1812. Echoing other buildings in which the Prince had a hand, the church incorporates in a compact beauty many elements of the Classic Revival style. It was at first entirely circular in design (perhaps inspired by the Duke's memory of similar buildings in North Germany): the pulpit was in the centre of the church with the pews arranged in concentric circles around it. To no one's surprise, from the beginning it has been known as "the Round Church."

Although fine as an abstract idea, the circular arrangement did not work in practice and in 1827 was modified to its current internal form. The building has remained untouched since, with the exception of the weathervane erected in 1835 to commemorate the appearance of Halley's Comet; the replacement in 1911 of the semi-circular entrance porch by a square one; and repairs necessitated by the Great Explosion of 1917.

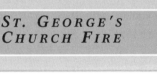

ST. GEORGE'S CHURCH FIRE

*I*n June 1994 St. George's Church was severely damaged by fire: about a third of the building was destroyed, including the distinctive cupola bell tower and the dome topped by the comet-shaped weathervane added in 1835. The local congregation decided to surmount this tragedy by raising the $6 million required to return the building to its former splendour. Many individual donors, along with federal and local governments, have contributed, as has a direct descendant of the original benefactors, Prince Charles.

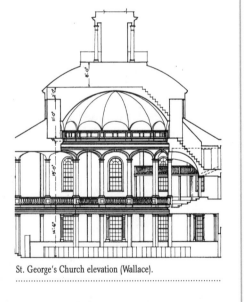

St. George's Church elevation (Wallace).

The church also offers an intriguing view into the brusque social practices of the time. It was the Royal Navy's place of worship, and naval officers, their families, and eminent citizens were seated in pews at the main level; servants and ordinary sailors occupied the galleries, which were stacked in theatre fashion all the way up to the celestial blue dome, where worshippers seated on rough benches peered out from under the arches. The social hierarchy is further reflected in the entrance porch, where the stairway has a separated tunnel for the use of those destined for the galleries.

On the north wall of the church is a **memorial tablet** to the astonishing Colonel Joseph Desbarres. Among his other accomplishments, he won distinction at the conquest of Louisbourg, was aide-de-camp to General Wolfe at the fall of Quebec—his navigation charts had made both campaigns possible—was a mentor to the renowned explorer Captain Cook, founded Sydney in Cape Breton, and died in 1824 at the advanced age of 103. He is buried under the church floor: the circular iron grating in the aisle next to the tablet is located directly over his tomb.

Opposite the church on Brunswick Street, at **2229** with its Scottish dormers, is an example of a Georgian North End cottage; it was built for two of Thomas Akins' aunts. Further along the street, at **2287** was built in 1863 in the style of an Italianate villa for Conrad West.

The **West House** is at 2319–23. This fine double home, built for two of the West brothers, is also known as the House of Angels, from the tranquil faces carved above the first storey windows.

On the next corner is the **Little Dutch Church**, the first church of German origin in Canada ("Dutch" being the insular English version of *Deutsches*). Built in 1756, it is the second oldest building in Halifax after St. Paul's Church.

In 1753 most of the recently arrived German settlers were moved to Lunenburg. Those remaining built a spartan meeting house of squared logs, adding a steeple in 1760 to hang the bell, which had been removed from the convent at Louisbourg. The building's congregation was Lutheran, so it has none of the classical style and ornamentation of the more established churches of the time. But the congregation made up for this, when in 1801, after forty years' hard saving and with the patronage of the British Royal Family, they moved down the street to their handsome new round church.

Just across the street, on the northwest corner, stood one of the three bastions built along Brunswick Street at the time of the American War of Independence. The bastions, along with the Citadel and Fort Needham, were designed to protect the dockyard against land attacks by American forces—possibly supported by rebellious Nova Scotians.

···· *Return to Cornwallis Street and turn left towards the harbour. Continue through the Barrington Street traffic intersection and turn left on Provo Wallis Street, the dockyard perimeter road.*

The Naval Dockyard

This, the oldest **naval dockyard** in North America, is steeped in history. For two centuries the ships of the Royal Navy, and later, the Canadian navy sailed from here into the North Atlantic: on the campaigns against Louisbourg and Quebec, Boston and New York, in two world wars to protect the great convoys sailing to Britain and Europe and—through two centuries—to cruise the seas in defence of the Halifax bastion.

····················
The Prince of Wales landing at Halifax (*Illustrated London News,* 1860).

SIR PROVO WALLIS: ADMIRAL OF THE FLEET

*T*he town produced many doughty sea dogs for the Empire, of whom several became admirals in the Royal Navy. But none compared to Provo Wallis, who was knighted, who rose to command Her Majesty's navy, and who died after ninety-six years' service in it.

In the eighteenth century, promotion in the Royal Navy depended on seniority. Wallis's father—the chief clerk at the dockyards—knew this and signed Provo on before his fourth birthday. So when young Provo reported for duty in 1804, he already had ten years' seniority. However, his own skills, dash, and courage were enough to take him to the top.

Provo's first taste of sea warfare came only a few months later, when his ship provoked a battle with a much larger French vessel. His exploits came to a wide audience in June 1813 after the famous encounter between HMS *Shannon* and the United States frigate *Chesapeake,* off Boston. In fifteen gory minutes it was all over, with the Royal Navy Ensign flying over the American ship and both captains critically wounded. As the *Chesapeake*'s Captain Lawrence was carried below, he uttered the famous, "Don't Give Up the Ship!"

The *Shannon*'s First Lieutenant had been killed in the battle, elevating Lieutenant Wallis, twenty-two years old, to his first command. Steering away from the menacing New England coast, the two vessels arrived five days later in Halifax. It had been a quiet Sunday, but as the news of the ships' appearance spread, St. Paul's Church emptied rapidly in mid-service as people ran to the harbour side—the excitement swelling with the news that a native son was the hero of the day.

At the end of the conflicts with the Americans and the French, Wallis's warfaring days were over. He spent his service years in a variety of increasingly elevated duties, including negotiating with the Emperor of Brazil and acting as aide-de-camp to Queen Victoria. He was knighted in 1860

and attained the navy's highest rank—Admiral of the Fleet—
in 1877.

Because of his service in the French wars, Sir Provo was
entitled to continue on full pay past the normal retirement
age. In 1886, when he was ninety-five years old, the lords of
the Admiralty politely asked him if he would consider
retiring; apart from anything else, he was holding up the
promotion of younger men. Wallis replied that he was quite
content with the current arrangement. The lords then pointed out, a little more bluntly, that as an Admiral on full pay
he was liable for sea duty. The old sea dog replied that nothing would give him greater pleasure than to return to sea in
Her Majesty's service—but his experience was in wooden
sailing ships, and he would know little of modern armoured
steamships. That ended the correspondence.

Laden with honours, he died in his hundredth year.
Shortly afterwards, four admirals were promoted to higher
rank.

After the failure in 1757 of an attack on Louisbourg, the
British realized the need for a fully established and outfitted
dockyard, and in 1759 land was bought below the German
church. Having earlier surveyed the harbour, Captain Cook in
1760-61 supervised some of the early construction work in the
dockyard.

By 1784 the **King's Yard**—complete with the Capstan House,
Sail Loft, Mast House, and numerous other buildings and
wharves—was flourishing. During the War of 1812 a nineteenth-
century peak of activity was reached, with about sixteen hundred
men servicing a fleet of 104 ships. Conditions for naval seamen at
this time were perhaps indicated by the presence, next to the
naval hospital, of a sizeable Lunatic House.

The only real threat to the yard—military or otherwise—came
in the 1870s, when the new Dominion government tried to com-
mandeer it for the Intercolonial Railway; these boarders were
successfully repelled. In fact the eighteenth-century dockyard
buildings remained intact and in use until the outbreak of the
Second World War, when, with the ruthless efficiency dictated by

the war, they were razed to the ground and replaced by modern structures. Today only a few buildings remain from the early years.

Note: As a modern naval base, the dockyard is not generally open to the public. However, a drive along the perimeter road—named Provo Wallis Street after one of Nova Scotia's naval heroes—gives a view of its extent and activities. At the jetties between the buildings you can glimpse Canadian navy vessels, and on occasion, vessels of NATO fleets in port after exercises in the North Atlantic. (These vessels may usually be visited on weekends.) Proceed northwards on Provo Wallis Street.

On your right, the wedge-shaped building is the **submarine shed** where submarines are refitted. The vessels are lifted out of the water by means of synchrolift equipment on the harbour side of the shed.

The modern structure just to the north of the submarine shed is the **Prince of Wales Building.** Opened in 1983 by the Prince and Princess of Wales, it was named in honour of two previous Princes of Wales who had arrived at a landing place here in 1860 and 1919, respectively. In 1951 Princess Elizabeth (great-granddaughter and niece, respectively, of the earlier Princes), accompanied by the Duke of Edinburgh, placed a plaque here, next to those commemorating the former Princes' arrivals.

···· *Continue along Provo Wallis Street under the bridge to Admiral's Gate.*

Next to Admiral's Gate is the **Royal Coat of Arms.** In 1959 the province donated it to the navy to celebrate the two hundredth anniversary of the founding of the King's Yard. Made of bronze, the piece weighs 3,000 lbs.

A few metres behind the gate can be glimpsed the oldest surviving buildings in the dockyard—**three residences** built in 1815 for the Surgeon, the Dispenser, and the Agent of the nearby naval hospital—and now used as senior officers' residences. Beyond the residences can be seen the modern red brick structure of **Maritime Command Headquarters.** The other survival from the early years is the 1767 clock from the old Sail Loft, which cannot be seen from the road; it ran continuously until the Great Explosion of 1917, and since repaired, continues to wind away the hours today. Situated on the northern edge of the dockyard, the Halifax Shipyards were established in 1918. Throughout the Second World War, they repaired naval and merchant ships damaged in the Battle of the Atlantic.

···· *Continue past Admiral's Gate around the curve, through the traffic intersection, and up the hill on North Street. Turn right on Gottingen Street and proceed to the Maritime Command Museum, on your right a short way along the street.*

Admiralty House (Maritime Command Museum)

Open year-round. April 1 to March 31: Monday to Friday, 10:00 A.M. –4:30 P.M.; summer hours vary. Free admission. Call (902)427-0550 (ext. 8250) for further information.

Admiralty House, a National Historic Site, was built between 1814 and 1818 as a residence for the British Admiral in command of the North American Station; it is now home to the Maritime Command Museum.

Appropriately enough, perhaps, the building's history has entailed some rough seas. Throughout the eighteenth century, admirals in Halifax had been forced to stay on their flagships

Reception of the new Governor-General at Admiralty House, 1860s.

when in the harbour. Later, cramped quarters were made available for them in the Naval Hospital, or a small allowance was provided for rental accommodation—although during the Napoleonic Wars even this was withdrawn as an inadmissible expense. After years of requests and petitions, money was finally approved for a residence. However, due to the difficulties in overseas communication in the age of sail, a stone building was constructed where the plans had called for a wooden one. Then work on the incomplete building was halted through lack of imperial money. Finally, the Nova Scotia Assembly contributed £1500, reasoning that the prestige of an Admiral's presence in the town was well worth the cost.

Barely a year after the residence was finished, the Admiral decided to move his squadron's headquarters to Bermuda. (The town's scuttlebutt had it that the Admiral had moved his squadron rather than give up the Berkshire hogs he was rearing at the back of Admiralty House and to which the neighbours were vociferously objecting.) The fleet still summered in Halifax, though, and the sturdy Georgian structure with its curving carriage drive and landscaped gardens were put to good use. Among the many garden parties and balls held here, in September 1848 the Earl of Dundonald gave a ball for six hundred uniformed and formally attired guests.

After the British naval and military forces were recalled to Britain in 1906, Admiralty House remained empty until the outbreak of the First World War when the Naval Hospital moved there. The large rooms were used as wards, the basement kitchen became the operating theatre, and an area of the basement was turned into a temporary morgue. After the war, the house became the naval wardroom and officers' mess—during the Second World War an average of six hundred meals a day were served, in six or seven shifts—continuing in this function until 1954.

The building has twice been seriously damaged—in 1857, when the magazine behind the Wellington Barracks blew up, and in the Great Explosion of 1917, when the roof was blown off and many of the ornate ceilings were brought down. It nevertheless retains its old dignity and many of its ornamental features: In the entrance hall and other rooms is richly moulded plasterwork in the ceiling friezes; there are several deeply polished mahogany doors; and throughout the house are original carved marble and wooden fireplace mantels.

In 1973 naval artefacts and memorabilia began to be assembled here, and in 1974 the Maritime Command Museum opened its doors to the public. Covering the British Royal Navy's presence in Halifax from 1759 and the Canadian navy's history from 1910, the museum displays a fascinating array of uniforms, ship models, and other items of naval interest; it also maintains a naval library and archives. In 1982 Admiralty House was proclaimed a National Historic Site.

···· *On leaving Admiralty House, turn right and continue northwards on Gottingen Street.*

On your right, a short way beyond Admiralty House, is the **Royal Canadian Regiment Gate,** memorializing that regiment's centenary in 1983 and its posting here from 1900. The regiment's battle honours are displayed on the gate's pillars. It was built in the 1850s as the gate to Wellington Barracks, which consisted of two large red brick imperial buildings, one for the officers, the second for "other ranks." The larger of the two, which was situated just behind the gate, was replaced by the current building during the Second World War, but the officers' mess remains, although not visible from the street. (No doubt fuelled by the memory of the confusion over the Admiralty House plans, it was rumoured that the barracks, with its tall open arches at ground level, had actually been intended for Bermuda.)

In 1857 the magazine on the harbour side of Wellington Barracks blew up, seriously damaging buildings in the area. In the immediate aftermath of the Great Explosion of 1917, the threat of a secondary explosion from the burning magazine sent hundreds of survivors streaming down Gottingen Street towards the Citadel and the South End—some fleeing as far as the woods on Point Pleasant Park.

···· *Proceed north along Gottingen Street past the traffic intersection at Young Street. After you see Fort Needham Park on your right, bear right onto Union Street at the end of the park; the parking area is to the left. (There is an alternative pedestrian entrance to the park at its southern end, on your right just past Young Street.)*

THE GREAT EXPLOSION OF 1917

*O*n a clear, bright morning in December 1917, the Belgian Relief ship *Imo*, moving from the Bedford Basin towards the harbour entrance, collided with the *Mont Blanc*, which was making her way towards the basin to join a convoy. The *Mont Blanc* carried 2,500 tons of TNT and inflammable chemicals. At the first signs of fire her crew abandoned ship and rowed furiously towards the Dartmouth shore, while the stricken vessel drifted to a flaming rest on the Halifax side of the harbour.

As brave men struggled to fight the ship's fires and move her away from the burning pier, workers and North End residents gathered on the waterfront and at the windows of their homes to watch. At 9:06 A.M. the *Mont Blanc* exploded with an engulfing roar and a shock wave that swept away all in its path.

After the blast came a deadly shower of red hot fragments of the ship. Rocks and boulders torn from the bottom of the harbour devastated the waterfront; the ship's half-ton anchor shank was hurled 5 km (3 mi.) to land across the Northwest Arm (see page 00). A tidal wave swept down the harbour, carrying people away and battering vessels, and was experienced as a powerful shock by ships many miles out to sea. The explosion's tremor was felt on Cape Breton, 240 km (150 mi.) away.

Under the mushroom-shaped cloud that rose 5 km (3 mi.) over Halifax, there was appalling carnage. Few people close to the explosion survived. Entire families were wiped out, either by the initial shock wave—which turned windows and other parts of houses into lethal missiles—or in the fires that followed, caused by overturned coal and wood stoves. In the sugar refinery and other factories there was total devastation. At Tufts Cove on the eastern side of the Narrows, the explosion simply erased the last Micmac encampment in the area. Over 2,000 people died and over 9,000 were injured. (By comparison, 650 people died in the famous Chicago Fire and San Francisco Earthquake combined.)

There were a number of miraculous escapes. Some people close to the explosion were entirely stripped of their clothing but left uninjured. A third officer on a ship near the *Mont Blanc* was snatched from the deck and in the midst of a huge cloud of wreckage was deposited—cut and bruised but otherwise unharmed—on the top of Fort Needham Hill. There were also many stories of stirring bravery and self-sacrifice. Doctors, nurses, and the military laboured,

sometimes for days without food or rest, to rescue survivors and to treat their injuries. There was the speedy and generous assistance from Massachusetts, to be followed by help from many other cities and states in North America and the British Commonwealth. (Massachusetts's generosity is commemorated to this day by the yearly delivery of a large tree to Boston at Christmas-time.)

Immediately after the explosion many thought that the city had been attacked by German Zeppelins, and in the following days and weeks a wave of revulsion against all things German swept the town. Haligonians of German descent were imprisoned, and some were stoned in the streets. When the area was resettled, German surnames, for so long predominant in the North End, had largely disappeared.

Fort Needham Park

In front of you on the crest of the hill is the Halifax Explosion **Memorial Bell Tower.** This dignified and heart-catching memorial directly overlooks the point in the Narrows where, at 9:06 A.M. on December 6, 1917, the Great Explosion erupted.

Before detonating, the burning *Mont Blanc* came to rest at a pier on the near shore adjoining Richmond Street; the gap between the sections of the monument and the footpath towards the harbour mark the old route of the street.

On a warm summer's day in 1985, the bell tower was dedicated as a memorial to the victims of the tragedy. The carillon of bells was donated by a survivor in honour of six members of her family who lost their lives in the explosion. Within the tower is a time capsule containing records and memorabilia of the event, to be opened at 9:06 a.m. on December 6, 2017.

Beyond the memorial, on your right is a **plaque to Captain Cook,** who, during his posting in Halifax, did much pioneering survey work of the harbour and elsewhere and was involved in the construction of the original naval yard. He later gained fame as the explorer of the South Pacific and Australia, opening up the continent for British colonisation.

The park gains its name from Fort Needham built in 1776 and long gone from the hill. It was situated where the tennis courts are now, and where, in the nineteenth century, British officers of the garrison played chukkas of polo.

The fort was a pentagonal earthen redoubt that enclosed two wooden barracks housing fifty men; it was surrounded by a ditch that was crossed by a bridge. Two 24-pounder cannon faced west to cover the isthmus to the mainland, while two faced south to join fire with the guns on Citadel Hill and cover the land approach to the dockyard. A detached blockhouse was built about 400 ft. northwest of the redoubt to cover the steep northern slope of the hill.

During the winter of 1807–08 both the redoubt and the blockhouse were hurriedly rebuilt in anticipation of an American attack. After 1825, a large masonry fort with an enclosed Martello tower was planned for the hill, also with the Americans in mind, but this fort—which would have rivalled the Citadel in size—was quietly forgotten as the Citadel's building costs mounted.

···· *From Fort Needham Park return along Gottingen Street towards the city.*

To the immediate west of Fort Needham Park is a section of the **Hydrostone area.** These buildings were completed in 1921 as part of the reconstruction in the wake of the Great Explosion. They were built partly of Hydrostone, the trade name of a grey heat-compressed block produced by a Chicago company.

The area around the hill was replanned by Thomas Adams, an Englishman who had settled in Canada. Recognizing the natural qualities of the area, he was able to implement some of the "Garden City" philosophy of town planners of the time. On boulevards carefully contoured to the hill, he built houses, many of which used a wood lattice and stucco design for the upper storey to give an English Village quality. The style is most visible as you glance down Young Street towards the business district.

On a field close to the hill, in 1819 Richard John Uniacke fought his duel with William Bowie, whose death resulted in the famous murder trial presided over by Uniacke's father, the Attorney General (see also Province House page 58).

···· *To conclude the tour, continue along Gottingen Street to the city. If you would like to take the extended tour, turn right on Young Street and continue below.*

Beyond the North End

This extended tour includes Fairview Cemetery—the burial ground of victims of the *Titanic* disaster—Bedford Basin, Mount Saint Vincent University, the D'Anville Expedition Memorial, and the Prince's Lodge rotunda. At the end of the tour, Hemlock Ravine Park—the site of the long-gone Prince's Lodge—offers a variety of enjoyable woodland walks.

A few cautionary words: Although the different points of interest in this section can be reached by bus, it is essentially a car tour. It is also one for the avid explorer: the locations include sights of real historical interest and, while directions are provided, a city map will be useful.

···· *Continue along Young Street past Agricola and Robie Streets and Kempt Road to the intersection at Windsor Street. Turn right on Windsor Street and continue along it to the traffic intersection at Connaught Avenue. Fairview Cemetery is on your left, a few metres further along Windsor Street.*

Fairview Cemetery is the burial place of 125 victims of the sinking of the *Titanic* in 1912; signposts indicate the route to the plot. The victims buried here were probably all First Class passengers as, following the social protocol of the time, the bodies of passengers from other classes were buried at sea. Also buried in the cemetery are many unidentified victims of the Great Explosion.

···· *Continue along Windsor Street to the traffic intersection and turn left towards Bedford.*

On your right, as you travel down the hill, is **Bedford Basin.** This deep anchorage captivated sailors who saw it: an eighteenth-century seaman reported that it was "large enough to hold the entire English navy." It has been well used over the years, never more so than in the two world wars, when it was blanketed with the merchant ships of the great British convoys about to depart on their often terrifying voyages across the North Atlantic.

···· *Continue along the Bedford Highway. On your left, about a kilometre past the first set of traffic lights, is Mount Saint Vincent University.*

Mount Saint Vincent University opened in 1873 as an academy where the Sisters of Charity trained novices and young sisters as teachers. By 1925 it was awarding its own degrees, becoming the only independent women's college in the British Commonwealth. Today men are admitted, although women still make up a high proportion of the enrolment. The university offers a broad variety of courses in association with Dalhousie University, the Technical University of Nova Scotia, and the Nova Scotia College of Art and Design.

On your right just past the university is a small park, the site of the **D'Anville Expedition Memorial.** This marks the location of a tragedy on these shores, when in 1745 a French fleet under D'Anville—bent on recapturing Louisbourg, to be followed by an attack on Boston—was devastated by storm and disease on the Atlantic voyage. The survivors of the shattered fleet landed around this point in the basin.

···· *Continue north along the Bedford Highway. About a kilometre past*

THE PRINCE'S LADY

*P*rince Edward built the lodge as a love nest for the arrival of a French woman who had been contracted as his mistress. From the middle class, she gloried under the name Alphonsine Julie Thérèse Bernadine de St. Laurent de Montgenet, Baronne de Fortisson—an aristocratic fiction designed to make her more palatable to the circles in which the Prince moved.

There were Haligonians who refused to go along with the charade, but in time the Prince's lady—better known as Madame Julie St. Laurent—became widely adored in the town, partly through their friendship with the open-minded Sir John and Lady Frances Wentworth but largely for her sensibility and refined beauty. The Prince's affection for her was equally clear; he spent much time at the lodge and had his cherished "telegraph" system extended here so that, as British Commander-in-Chief in North America, he could keep in touch with his responsibilities.

Prince's Lodge rotunda *(Canadian Illustrated News)*.

The fairy tale had a bittersweet ending. King George III's errant sons were all finally called to account, and the Prince was forced to leave Julie. Fulfilling his royal destiny, he successfully fathered an heir to the throne, the future Queen Victoria.

the D'Anville Memorial, the road curves to the left around Birch Cove; on your right, a few hundred metres beyond Birch Cove, is the Prince's Lodge rotunda. Turn left at Kent Avenue opposite the rotunda.

The **Prince's Lodge rotunda** (now a private home owned by the provincial government) is the only surviving building of the lodge built by Prince Edward, who lived here between 1794 and 1800. The rotunda, patterned after the "temples" built in the gardens of eighteenth-century English aristocrats, was used as a music pavilion. The Prince's own musicians, drawn from the regimental band of the Royal Fusiliers, played at the soirees. With the rotunda's gilded ball glowing in the afternoon sun over the splendidly uniformed guests, the building must have seen some dazzling occasions.

···· *Continue along Kent Avenue to the Hemlock Ravine Park parking lot, to your left at the end of the road.*

A few metres into **Hemlock Ravine Park** is a heart-shaped ornamental pond. This was excavated at Prince Edward's common, and apart from the rotunda, it is the only surviving element of the lodge. For the edification of royal guests, a pagoda was built on a small island in the middle of the pond and wind chimes were hung from the surrounding trees.

The lodge itself, a two-storey wooden Italianate building, was situated on the hill above and to the north of the pond. In addition to the main villa and kitchen were Chinese style "temples" and meandering paths, which romantic legend has it spelt out the name "Julie."

···· *To return to the city on the Bedford Highway, the Barrington Street route is best; it offers a fine vista of Bedford Basin and the harbour, passes Seaview Park (the site of Africville), and is the simplest route.*

···· *As you come to the end of the Bedford Highway (at the large traffic intersection), watch for signs to Barrington Street and follow these to the downtown area.*

A few hundred metres before the MacKay Bridge you pass **Seaview Park,** the site of Africville. The park commemorates this old community, levelled in the 1960s and a potent symbol from the city's past. To enter the park, turn left at the entrance a few hundred metres after driving under the bridge.

···· *From the park, continue along Barrington Street to the downtown area.*

South End

Tour 6 includes sights—in particular Dalhousie University, the University of King's College, and St. Mary's University—which do not fit easily into a short walking tour.

Extending from Citadel Hill to Point Pleasant Park, the South End offers a variety of unique and absorbing points of interest, from the many fine examples of Georgian and Victorian military or domestic architecture to the gracious Public Gardens and the Nova Scotia Museum. Along with the other areas of the city, the South End has also witnessed some dramatic historical events.

The bandstand, Public Gardens (L. B. Jenson).

Introduction

Note: Tour 6 begins on facing page.

In the early years, the area was an expanse of swamp, scrub, and pine forest, well beyond the settlement's log palisades; later, a few roads were cut through these wild lands, leading to the forts and sea batteries. In time, fields for cultivation and grazing were cleared, to be followed by small homes and private estates.

Many of the more humble dwellings were built close to the old town in the first half of the nineteenth century—the cottages, quarters, and townhouses of merchants, military men, tradesmen, and artisans. These buildings were built in the Georgian style, fashionable during the period which extended over the reigns of George II, George III, and George IV—roughly from the mid-eighteenth to the mid-nineteenth century—and for some years beyond.

Fine examples of these Georgian style homes may be seen in the old South End area once called Schmidt Ville. Although modest in size and detail when compared to the city's grand Georgian public buildings, they represent a rich architectural style and tradition of their own—stemming from British forms handed down from medieval times and from eighteenth- and early nineteenth-century Scottish and New England design trends. These different styles were blended in a local interpretation that gives the city's domestic architecture a unique character.

The Victorian heritage is strongly represented, perhaps most strikingly by the Public Gardens but also in the dignified residential areas. The South End—as the city's fashionable section in the late nineteenth and early twentieth centuries—has numerous Victorian buildings, many of which were constructed after the great Nova Scotian shipping boom of the mid 1800s. These are particularly appealing for someone with an eye for architectural style: Second Empire, Gothic and Queen Anne Revival, Eclectic, and even Italianate styles are all represented here.

Spread among the residential areas are many public institutions, including hospitals and universities, and green amid the encroaching concrete, the South End still maintains a few pieces of its rustic past where portions of the old South Common—once used for the grazing of cattle and by the military for reviews and manoeuvres—survive.

Note: The description of South End buildings in this section owes much to Elizabeth Pacey's Georgian Halifax, *which offers a wealth of*

insight and detail that cannot be covered in this tour and which is
warmly recommended for further reading and exploration.

....
START TOUR

Start and end point: Royal Artillery Park on Sackville Street
between Brunswick and Queen Streets (three minutes' walk
south from the Old Town Clock.
Time: One to three hours.

Royal Artillery Park

Behind the wrought-iron fence on Sackville Street are two modest
white buildings used originally by officers of the Royal Artillery.
They are the only surviving examples in Halifax of the many
wooden officers' quarters and barracks, which once studded the
town.

The Royal Regiment of Artillery manned the fortress's guns
from the founding in 1749 to the British departure in 1906.
(Unlike the long procession of infantry regiments, which each
garrisoned the town for a few years only.) In the mid-1790s,
Prince Edward built a barracks for his artillery just to the east of
the park, and a few years later, the current buildings were
constructed.

On the left is the **Commanding Officer's Residence** (originally "Quarters for the Commanding Officer and Adjutant of the
Royal Artillery"). It was completed in 1805 by the Commanding
Royal Engineer, Captain Fenwick, who left many intriguing
details of its construction: the wall plaster, for example, was
made from a mixture of ninety-two hogsheads of lime and sixty
bushels of cow hair, while the design included a "Necessary
House" with a "Stone Drain for Carrying Off the Nuisances." Also
of interest is the fact that although the building was designed for
the commanding officer and the adjutant, there is no evidence
that the adjutant was ever given permission to move in.

The residence was always used by either the Royal Artillery or
the Royal Engineers, or after 1906, by the officers of the Royal
Canadian Artillery and by the General Officer Commanding the
military district.

The building on the right is the **Officers' Mess** (originally the
"Royal Artillery Officers' Quarters and Mess Room"), completed

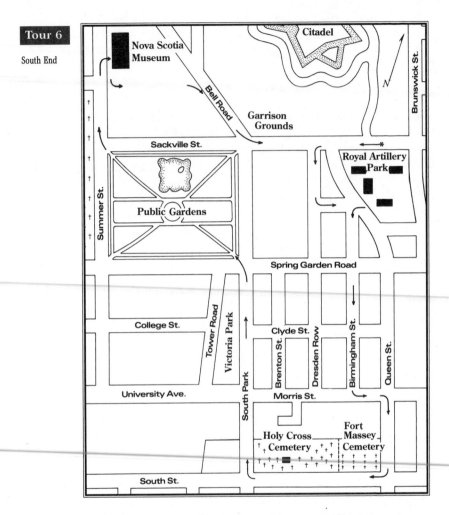

in 1816 by Colonel Gustavus Nicholls, the Royal Engineer who later designed the Citadel. To accommodate the new building, the western end of the park was enlarged in 1812, giving Queen Street its curious curve. When completed, the building housed three Royal Artillery subalterns and their mess and serves as a mess to this day.

···· *Walk west (away from the harbour) and cross Queen Street to the corner of Sackville Street and Dresden Row.*

Bollard House, on the corner, was originally a conventional symmetrical Georgian house. When Dresden Row was extended in 1835, the Queen Street swerve brought on by the enlargement of the park for the Officers' Mess produced a trapezoidal-shaped lot. The owner was unwilling to lose the extra space, and the house was expanded into its current mildly eccentric shape. Named for the shipwright Charles Bollard, in later years the house gained a minor reputation due to his three spinster daughters, who untiringly chased fascinated artists away.

···· *Proceed south (away from Citadel Hill) on Dresden Row.*

Below the Bollard House on Dresden Row is a small array of **Georgian houses,** including examples at 1589, 1579, and 1577-1569. The unpretentious townhouse at 1579 has several indicators of Georgian style, including the narrow gabled dormers and pitched roof. Inside, the rooms are small, with a limited entrance hall and narrow staircase.

Before turning off Dresden Row, glance back along the line of buildings towards the Citadel. Particularly in a mist that blurs the modern edges, one sees the town as it was in the nineteenth century: modest homes jostling together at the base of the Imperial hill.

···· *Turn left on Artillery Place and proceed one block to Queen Street.*

As you approach Queen Street, on your left across the street in Royal Artillery Park is a large Victorian red brick building. Constructed as the Artillery and Engineer Officers' Quarters in 1903, a few years before the imperial garrison left Halifax, it is used as officers' quarters to this day.

Cambridge Library
Although the library is not generally open to the public, appointments may be made to view or use it.

In front of you, the smallish red brick building is the **Cambridge Library,** completed in 1886. This military library is a sturdy example of the late nineteenth-century British Army cantonment style found in garrison towns across the Empire. It was named for the Duke of Cambridge, the British Commander-in-Chief through most of Victoria's reign, who reportedly appreciated the compliment. Surprisingly large inside, it has hosted many

High Teas and dances, in addition to its normal functions.

The library's root collection contains books purchased with money from the Castine Fund. When the occupying British forces withdrew from Maine after the War of 1812, they brought with them the funds collected in customs and other duties at Castine, and although some of the money went to the founding of Dalhousie University, the Earl of Dalhousie also put aside £1,000 for a garrison library "for the use of military and naval officers," a small salutation to his benefactors.

Modelled after the garrison library at that other imperial stronghold, Gibraltar, the collection was at first a cross-section of what the genteel Victorian officer would be reading—upright and somewhat middlebrow. It was enriched in 1864 when the books from the Corfu Garrison Library were shipped to Halifax at the end of the British occupation of the island. Among the many items of military interest are copies of the Duke of Wellington's Orders and the Army Lists of the day.

···· *Turn down Birmingham Street and proceed one block to Spring Garden Road. Note, on your left, the row of small Georgian and Victorian buildings.*

Currently a popular shopping area, **Spring Garden Road** has some fascinating links with the past: among them, in the eighteenth century its eastern end marked the South Gate which gave entry to the settlement huddled behind its blockaded walls; in a small plot in the old Governor's garden the Indians buried the hatchet with the settlers; on the corner of Queen Street, the Duke of Kent built Bellevue, a mansion for his Commanding General; and during the later years of the nineteenth century, on Sundays and holidays the road was a fashionable Haligonian promenade.

···· *Cross Spring Garden Road and continue one block along Birmingham Street.*

Schmidt Ville

The area bounded by Spring Garden Road and Morris Street west of Queen Street was originally called Pedley's Fields, after James Pedley who acquired the land in 1781. Pedley bequeathed the land to his daughter Elizabeth who had married a Captain Schmidt, a loyal and courageous German officer of His Majesty's

Royal Foreign Artillery. When, as a widow in 1830, Elizabeth Schmidt divided the lands into small lots for sale, the area became known as Schmidt Ville. In honour of her father's birthplace, she named one street Birmingham; in memory of her husband's ancestry she named another Dresden Row.

In this section of Birmingham Street are several relatively unaltered Georgian style homes. These include numbers **1351, 1341, 1336/1338** (described below), **1335, 1329/1333** (described below), **1326, 1322, 1318/1320** (described below), and **1316.** Many of these are examples of mirror-image cottages, a British style that developed in the early 1700s. In general, these cottages shared one roof and a common chimney, although in contrast to the home country's stone cottages, Halifax's buildings were influenced by New England styles and are of colourfully painted wood.

Georgian home, South End.
....

The cottages at **1336/1338,** with their separated chimneys and centrally placed doors, give the sense of one large home, as does the gable dormer above the doors. The oriel, or five-sided dormer, on each side is of Scottish descent, a distinctive feature of the Halifax Georgian character.

Numbers **1329/1333** also use Scottish dormers, but in this case the doors are at opposite ends of the building, creating more of an impression of separateness. The prominence of the dormers suggests that the house was completed soon after the Schmidt Ville subdivision, when they were most popular.

The rustic dwellings at **1318/1320** were built in Pedley's Fields before the subdivision and are among the oldest dwellings in the area (coins dating to 1814 were recently recovered from beneath the floorboards). The gabled dormers are a variation of the Scottish type; only one room deep, the entire building is spare and compact, with low doors, small windows, and narrow staircases.

···· *If you would like to make a short detour to view further Georgian style homes on Morris Street and Dresden Row continue immediately below—if not, turn left on Morris Street and continue at* ☛.

···· At the end of Birmingham Street, turn right on Morris Street and walk one block to Dresden Row.

There is a profusion of Georgian houses on Morris Street. In this area, numbers **5610, 5619, 5621, 5628,** and **5632** are good examples. From the corner of Morris and Dresden Row, on the opposite side of the street, four dormered houses in a row can be seen.

···· Turn right on Dresden Row.

Number 1317 is an example of the Classic Revival style, which was very popular in the United States after the War of Independence. This compact house with its triangular pediment is built in mansion style, echoing the refinement of grander classical buildings in its formal symmetry.

Number 1328/1332 reflects on a cottage scale the Neoclassical style so fashionable in the late 1700s. An unpretentious building, it reflects a simple elegance. Further examples of the local Georgian style may be seen at 1338 and 1342/1346 Dresden Row.

···· Return to Morris Street and turn left.
☛ Continue along Morris Street to the intersection and turn right on Queen Street.

Note: Further east down Morris Street are several fine examples of Georgian townhouses at 5274, 5270 and 5248. The dressed-stone Crofton-Uniacke House (at 5248), built in 1807 for the son of Attorney General Richard Uniacke, is constructed of solid granite—the only one of its kind in the city.

Along Queen Street at **1257, 1247, 1239–1243, 1229,** and **1211–1215** are several Georgian homes. Of a later period, number 1266 is an example of the so-called Second Empire school of Victorian architecture, popularised by Napoleon III. Numbers. 1211–1215 are another interesting pair of mirror-image cottages, showing the elevated entries, which were so popular in early Georgian Halifax.

On your right as you approach South Street is the **Fort Massey Cemetery.** It was originally the burying ground for the

*I*n 1844 the newspapers were full of details about the capture and conviction of four pirates in the sensational *Saladin* case. After their conviction they were brought to a small hill on the South Common (where the Victoria General Hospital now stands) and publicly hanged.

On a bright, summery day, the men, escorted by the King's Royal Regiment with fixed bayonets, were marched to the scaffold. A great throng of townspeople turned out for the occasion, held "at a proper distance" by the red-coated soldiers of the 52nd Regiment of Foot. As the pirates mounted the scaffold a wave of sentimentality swept the crowd, brought on by one of the condemned men who "alone seemed indifferent to his awful situation. He stood perfectly erect and gazed around on the vast assemblage, on the green fields, the blue sky and the ocean before him."

After the execution, two of the bodies were placed in the recently completed Chapel of Our Lady of Sorrows across South Park Street before burial in a small unconsecrated corner of the cemetery; the others were taken, unsentimentally, to the Poor House graveyard.

fort constructed south of the town just after the American War of Independence. The fort's main feature was a blockhouse, located at the junction of Queen and South Streets; this commanded a ravine below, through which the Fresh Water River flowed from its source in the Common swamp down to the harbour, where sailors filled their vessels' water casks. The cemetery, where, as Thomas Raddall put it, "with musketry and muffled drum imperial soldiers buried their dead," continues as a burial ground for military men to this day.

Diagonally opposite is the handsome **Fort Massey United Church.** Built at the peak of Empire in 1871, it incorporates a number of the Gothic architectural features popular at the time.
···· *Turn right on South Street.*

A short way along the block the regimented rows of grave-stones shift to the more variegated ones of **Holy Cross Cemetery**. Solidly placed on the hillock overlooking the cemetery is the Chapel of Our Lady of Sorrows; the chapel was entirely constructed and painted between dawn and dusk on what must have been a very warm day in August 1843. A few weeks later, according to a contemporary report, around fifty thousand people—an enormous turnout for the times—attended the blessing of the chapel and cemetery.

···· *Turn right on South Park Street.*

Across South Park Street from the cemetery is a small park, the southernmost remainder of what, in the nineteenth century, were many acres of Common land.

···· *Continue to the traffic intersection at Morris Street.*

Note: One block to your left Morris Street becomes University Avenue. A few minutes' walk westwards along University Avenue will take you to the Public Archives of Nova Scotia, Dalhousie University, and the University of King's College. (See Additional Points of Interest on page 161–63.)

Diagonally to your left across, the Morris Street intersection, is the modest **Victoria Park**, a further remnant of the South Common. At the southern end of the park is a stone cairn, which memorializes Sir William Alexander who attempted to colonize Nova Scotia with Scots in the 1620s. Although he did not succeed in this venture, he nevertheless contributed the province's name and its flag: the Lion of Scotland surmounting the Cross of St. Andrew. The cairn is made of stones from Sir William's Menstrie Castle in Scotland.

At the north end of the park is a statue of Robbie Burns, another commemoration of the Scottish contribution to Nova Scotia; it was donated to the city by the North British Society in 1919. The bronze panels on the four sides of the native granite pedestal represent scenes from some of Burns's poems—"Tam o' Shanter," "Auld Lang Syne," "To a Mouse," and "The Cotter's Saturday Night."

Diagonally to your right as you arrive at the intersection is the **Lord Nelson Hotel.** The city's most modern and luxurious hotel when it was built in 1927, it sustains an old-world dignity and ambience today. Portraits of the great naval hero, Lord Nelson, and his battles on many of the walls and rooms with such names as the Regency and Imperial Ballroom, the Georgian and Victory Lounges, and the HMS *Bellisle* Function Room, all evoke the city's long association with the Empire and its navy.

During the Second World War, the hotel was a popular watering-place for military and naval officers, who would sometimes climb to the roof to watch the great convoys as they began their hazardous journey across the Atlantic. In more peaceful times it has hosted many dignitaries, including Princess (now Queen) Elizabeth during her Canadian tour.

···· *Cross the intersection to the Public Gardens.*

The Public Gardens

The Halifax **Public Gardens** are the oldest original Victorian public gardens in Canada and probably the finest in North America. In a relatively small compass the gardens offer a rich assortment of native and exotic trees, flowers, and shrubs—and also host a variety of birds, from the Common Grackle and House Sparrow to swans and gulls, Black and Mallard Ducks, and

Main gate,
Public Gardens
(L. B. Jenson).

CHURCHILL VISITS THE PUBLIC GARDENS

*I*n 1943, on his top-secret trip to the Quebec Conference to plan the D-Day landings with President Roosevelt, Winston Churchill passed through Halifax accompanied by Lord Louis Mountbatten and the British Chiefs of Staff. On his way home, Churchill was able to spend some time in the city. After visiting the Citadel and the Northwest Arm, the motorcade drew up at the main gate to the Public Gardens.

Accompanied by his entourage and puffing on the inevitable cigar, Churchill strode to the pond, where he paused briefly to admire a model of the Cunarder *Queen Mary* (the ship that had brought him from England)—and to acknowledge two surprised airmen who leapt to their feet and saluted, their half-eaten ice cream cones held smartly upright in their left hands.

Word of Churchill's presence spread quickly, and a crowd burgeoned around him. He stopped to chat with some of the gardens' workers and to pass out cigars (some of which may still be mouldering on Nova Scotian mantel-pieces or in attics—the newspapers headlined the incident, "Cigars Won't Be Smoked." On the way back to the cars, he encountered two small boys leaning over the stone bridge near the main gate: he pinched one of them playfully on the thigh; but the youngster—after glancing up briefly without recognition—returned to the more urgent mission of watching for fish.

As the entourage climbed into their cars, a small traffic jam developed on the corner of South Park and Spring Garden when a tram conductor caught a glimpse of Churchill, leapt into the street, threw his cap into the air, and led the passengers in three cheers. Beaming with plea-sure, the great man flashed them his famous V sign and drove off for a visit to Point Pleasant Park, before boarding a British battleship for the dangerous voyage home.

the occasional hawk. In summer, as for over a century, band concerts are presented from the bandstand every Sunday afternoon.

The Victorians loved the outdoors. The heart and romance of that age, glimpsed in the crumbling forts and rusting cannon around the harbour, have been held intact in the green and spacious world of the gardens—as if "a chord of Elgar's *Pomp and Circumstances* had been metamorphosed into hedges and flower beds," as one writer put it. Today, as when they opened in 1875 at the full flush of the Empire, the gardens are an ordered and loving blend of geometric flower beds, serpentine walks, exotic trees, and nineteenth-century statuary.

The gardens are laid out on a part of what was originally a large swamp, dotted with pools and drained by rivers. Micmac tradition has it that their forefathers hunted wild duck on the pond. The area became part of the Common, and the pond came to be known—with the gloomy sentimentality of the time—as Griffin's Pond, for an Irishman, who in the 1830s, was hanged on its eastern edge.

In 1872, Richard Power was appointed superintendent of the gardens. Previously the foreman of the Duke of Devonshire's estate at Lismore Castle in Ireland, he transformed the land from the swampy wasteland to its current form.

To commemorate Queen Victoria's Golden Jubilee in 1887, a bandstand was erected in the centre of the park, and statues of the Greek goddesses Ceres, Diana, and Flora were put up at various points; the bandstand was immediately used for weekly concerts by the fine bands from the Royal Navy's warships and the garrison regiments. Ten years later, for the Queen's Diamond Jubilee, the nymph fountain was built to the west of the pond. As if to counterbalance the feminine statuary and to signal the imminent decline of the Empire, in 1903 the Boer War fountain was installed as a memorial to the Haligonians who lost their lives in that war.

···· *Leave the Public Gardens by the northwest gate (beyond the nymph fountain, at the diagonally opposite corner of the gardens from the main gate.)*

On the other side of Summer Street—beneath the cemetery and the modern hospital—is **Camp Hill**, a rise that lay on the edge of the old Common. Frequently used for military encampments, in 1776 General Howe's bitter and defeated troops pitched their tents here and on the Common after George Washington manoeuvred Howe out of Boston; it again served as an emergency campsite when troops were moved from infected barracks during the cholera epidemic of 1834. The gentle hill gave the designers of the Citadel some severe headaches: if an enemy were to capture and mount his cannon on it, the hill would be quite close enough to cause serious and perhaps fatal damage to the fort.

The **Camp Hill Cemetery**, begun in the 1830s, has been, from Queen Victoria's reign, a principal burying place for Haligonians. Joseph Howe, the great Nova Scotian politician, is buried here beneath a modest headstone.

···· *Cross Sackville Street to the opposite corner.*

Dominated by the Citadel, the **Wanderer's Ground**—on the right—was for many years part of the Common used for drilling and reviewing the troops of the garrison. In 1886 the Wanderers Amateur Athletic Club leased the ground from the city, and since then competitive games of cricket and rugby were played against garrison, Royal Navy, and the Maritimes teams. The grounds are now used for the more recent sports of baseball and football.

···· *Continue along Summer Street to the Nova Scotia Museum.*

The **Nova Scotia Museum,** the centre of the provincial museum system, presents exhibits on Nova Scotian themes from prehistoric times to the present day. It originated as part of the Halifax Mechanics Institute in 1831 (when Joseph Howe gave the inaugural address) and stands on part of the city's old Common land.

In the galleries are permanent exhibits on geological history, plant and animal life, and freshwater and ocean fish. There are also exhibits on the artefacts of the Micmac—including a large collection of quillwork—and on local furniture and pottery. On the main floor are exhibits of local, national, and international interest that change approximately four times a year.

Open seven days a week, shorter hours on Sundays, in off-season. Closed Mondays and small admission charge from June 1 to October 15. Call (902)424-7353 for further information.

Prince Arthur reviewing the Halifax Garrison on the Common *(Illustrated London News,* 1869).

···· *As you leave the museum, turn left and continue past the museum parking lot. Then turn left along the footpath that runs next to the Wanderer's Ground fence and continue past the Halifax Mounted Police and Bengal Lancers stables. Turn right onto Bell Road and walk towards the traffic lights.*

Across the street, just past the single-storey militia buildings (constructed during the Second World War) are the **Garrison Grounds.** An innocuous-looking sports field now, in the eighteenth and early nineteenth century, this ground was used by British military commanders to shoot their defaulters—"behind the hill," as was said.

In this century the grounds have seen more heartening events. In 1939, just before the outbreak of the Second World War, King George VI and Queen Elizabeth (the current Queen's mother) were feted here at a pageant of welcome, with a huge crowd of Haligonians spread across the hill in the summer heat. Continuing to the present and following a time-honoured tradition, members of the Royal Family—most recently Princesses

SUNDAY AFTERNOON ON THE COMMON

*U*ntil the twentieth century the Common land was used by the garrison for drill practice, manoeuvres, and parades. On Sundays, the townspeople turned out in large numbers to watch the Governor and his suite review the garrison; in the period of the early 1820s from which the following report comes, the garrison consisted of three full infantry regiments, three artillery batteries, and a large corps of engineers.

"After dinner, when the weather permitted it, the community streamed out to the Common to see a review of the troops or Garrison. There the great and the little were found in their holiday attire, the wealthy in their carriages and the poorer orders on shank's mare.

At the west side of the Common, somewhere about where the old race course ran, the Royal Standard flaunted its gay fold, and clustered around it on either side were the carriages of the wealthy, for thither came the Governor (then a General) with his staff, and around those luminaries clustered the moths and the millers as they have ever done and ever will do. At about half past four His Excellency and his suite, their gay plumes waving in the air, and their bright uniforms flashing in the summer light, made their appearance, and galloping down to the stand took their position.

The several bands all played the National Anthem, and the business of the review proceeded. A march round at slow step with a salute and another at quick step without it, and the review was over, and the Common in a very brief space of time restored to the quiet which had pervaded it some two hours before."

(From Peter Lynch, Early Reminiscences of Halifax, *read before the Nova Scotia Historical Society, February 3, 1887.)*

Anne and Margaret—have reviewed and presented new colours to Nova Scotian regiments here. When not hosting royal personages and parades, the grounds are used for football and sometimes rugby matches, as well as regular rock concerts. By now the old ghosts must be well exorcised.

···· *Cross South Park Street and continue along Sackville Street to the tour's end point at Royal Artillery Park.*

Additional Points of Interest

Beyond the area covered in Tour 6, the South End includes residential areas, universities, and other public institutions. This section describes some of these additional points of interest.

As the city's fashionable suburb in the late nineteenth and early twentieth centuries, the dignified residential neighbourhoods of the South End hold many examples of the Halifax Victorian heritage. One of the interesting stretches is along **Young Avenue** (the extension of South Park Street to Point Pleasant Park). Lined with the houses of Halifax Brahmins, in the late nineteenth century Haligonian mothers would parade their daughters along this elegant avenue, so that British officers of the garrison and navy riding to Point Pleasant Park would be sure to notice them, acknowledged by a passing bow.

About ten minutes' walk along University Avenue, west of South Park Street, is **Dalhousie University.** Founded in 1818 by the Earl of Dalhousie with money from the Castine Fund, its original location was at the north end of the Grand Parade (where the City Hall is now). With a current student body of approximately ten thousand, the university offers courses in a broad variety of disciplines and enjoys an international reputation.

The university occupies over 24 ha (60 acres) of the old Studley estate of Sir Alexander Croke who, as Judge of the Halifax Court of Vice-Admiralty in the early 1800s, did very well from the prizes brought into the harbour by privateers. Sections of the dry stone walls that surrounded the estate may be seen on Coburg Road and on South Street.

Affiliated with Dalhousie University and occupying the same campus, the **University of King's College** is Canada's oldest English-speaking university. It has a distinguished pedigree: modelled after Oxford University in England, it was founded in 1789 by a charter from George III. (The founding Anglican Loyalists, who had moved to Nova Scotia after the American Revolution, were handing on the flame of King's College in New York—chartered by George II in 1756; after the Revolution the New York college became Columbia University.) Emulating the ancient English university, the college has an excellent academic reputation and has produced more Rhodes Scholars per capita than any other Canadian university.

King's College has shared the Studley Campus with Dalhousie University since 1929. For several years during the Second World War, the college's Italian Renaissance buildings were converted to military use as HMCS Kings, training officers for sea duty in the Royal Canadian Navy.

Also situated on University Avenue, the **Public Archives of Nova Scotia** occupy a modern building, complete with solar panels for ecologically sound heating. In existence since 1857, the archives contain—and make available to researchers and the public—government and private papers of permanent historical value for Nova Scotia. Among the many documents in the collections are copies of the *Halifax Gazette,* in 1752 the first paper to be published in Canada.

Closed Mondays. Open weekdays from 8:30 A.M. Weekends, Saturday 9:00 A.M.–5:00 P.M.; Sunday 1:00 P.M.–5:00 P.M. Call (902)424-6060 for further information.

Situated largely between University Avenue and South Street is a major medical complex that includes the Victoria General Hospital, Grace Maternity Hospital, and the Izaak Walton Killam Hospital for children.

One block west of South Park Street at Inglis (between Tower Road and Robie Street) is **St. Mary's University,** the oldest English-speaking Roman Catholic university in Canada. Founded in 1802, it was originally a college located at the corner of Spring Garden Road and Barrington Street, adjoining St. Mary's Basilica. The university moved to its current Gorsebrook Campus in 1951 and is now a public university welcoming students of all races, creeds, and nationalities.

The campus grounds were originally part of Gorsebrook, the estate of Enos Collins; the estate's original capped stone wall may be seen along Tower Road south of Inglis Street. Reputedly the richest man in Canada when he died, Collins had made his start in the late eighteenth century as a privateer on the Spanish Main and in the French West Indies. (It is of interest that the estates on which the two major South End universities were built were originally acquired, at least in part, from the huge profits made in privateering.)

In 1900 the Halifax Golf Club leased part of the estate; the club's guests included officers of the Royal Navy, who were known to bring their ships' bands along to entertain them as they played.

.... *Point Pleasant Park is a few minutes' walk south along Tower Road from the St. Mary's campus.*

McNabs Island

Tour 7 covers McNabs Island. Lying at the harbour mouth, it is a largely unspoilt natural wilderness with an abundance of bird, animal, and plant life. It offers delightful walks through the woods and along the shoreline and a variety of spots for relaxation and picnicking. Fine views of the harbour, historic Georges Island, and the shipping terminals can be viewed on the ferry trip to the island.

Be sure to wear good walking shoes and to bring a warm jacket, as the temperature drops on the open water and sometimes on the island. You might also consider bringing your own supplies—except for the Island Tea Garden, there are no sources of food and water on the island. Please note too that the old forts and sea batteries are in a semi-ruined state, and care should be taken when exploring them.

From its earliest years a popular recreation area, the island has also figured large in the human events played out in the harbour. For many years the Micmac summered here, in the seventeenth century the French used it for a fishing station, while—seeing its commanding position in the main harbour channel—the British found a key role for the island the fortress system.

Halifax from McNabs Island (Eager, 1839).

Introduction

Note: Tour 7 begins on page 166.

McNabs Island has perhaps a longer human history than any spot in Halifax. Long before the harbour became important to the competitive Europeans, the Micmac held their spring celebrations here and spent the summers relaxing on the hospitable island with its rich offshore fishing.

In the 1600s the French came upon it, set up a fishing station and began missionary work among the Indians; a French priest was buried here in that century. By 1711 the French military had their eye on the island and planned to build a fortified town here—until a treaty with the British obliged them to put their Fortress of Louisbourg in a much inferior Cape Breton location.

After the British arrived they named it Cornwallis Island after their expedition's leader. Then in 1782 the entire island was purchased for "one thousand pounds sterling" by Peter McNab, an ex-Royal Navy lieutenant. He and his descendants cleared the land and farmed it for many years (a literary portrayal of their adventures survives in Thomas Raddall's novel *Hangman's Beach*).

Within a few years of the town's settlement, Haligonians discovered the island's scope for pleasure and recreation. They put it to passionate use. In the 1780s, George III's son Prince William and his raffish companions held chowder parties here; in 1790— in the heyday of the Halifax coffee houses—the enterprising Mary Roubalet built a "house of entertainment" named the Mansion House to host summer tea parties; and, over the long peaceful summers of the nineteenth century, townspeople descended on the island in the thousands, in sailing craft, paddle boats and steamers—and, in at least one case, a warship—to picnic, dance, play games, or just cavort in the rich harbour air.

In 1839 Samuel Cunard was feted by his fellow Haligonians at an immense picnic on the island after obtaining the first mail steamer contract from the British Admiralty, thereby ushering in the age of steamship travel. It was a gala occasion. In a flag-bedecked pavilion, buckets of clams and oysters were provided for the guests, there were two huge frosted cakes in the shape of pyramids surmounted by flags and ample supplies of liquid refreshment for the many toasts to be drunk in celebration of the event, and of their soon-to-be-famous townsman.

In 1869 Prince Arthur attended the annual Gathering of the Scottish Clans here, landing from the appropriately named HMS *Mullet.* That day the townspeople made their way to the island on the steamer *Micmac,* royally accompanied by the music of the regimental band of the 78th Highlanders (the same regiment that is represented at the Citadel today, courtesy of the Canadian Parks Services). For years the *Micmac* plied between town and island; on one summer's evening in 1873 the ship's smokestack toppled over, spewing smoke and steam (but injuring no one), causing what one newspaper described as "the most hurried disembarkation that ever took place in this city."

The military saw that the island—situated at the harbour mouth like a stopper in the mouth of a bottle—might be used to close off the harbour to enemy shipping. In 1814 they built the last of Halifax's five Martello Towers on Mauger Beach, but the island only came into its own as a site for sea batteries after the introduction of the longer-range rifled guns in the 1860s, when a strong fort was constructed at Ives Point and the "stopper" could be well and truly closed. As weapons became ever more power-ful, and it became necessary to stop enemy ships further from the harbour, the island's role grew in importance. At the turn of the century, Forts Hugonin and McNab were constructed, the lat-ter serving through both world wars. During the Second World War Strawberry Battery was built just south of Mauger Beach.

Today, in addition to the historic points of interest, its wildlife and plants, and its many attractions for ramblers and picnickers, the island has become popular with a new generation—offering both the experience of a sea-swept wilderness close to the heart of a modern city and a deep glimpse into an engrossing past.

....

START TOUR

Start and end point: Cable Wharf along Water Street. Call Tourism Halifax at (902)421-8736 for McNabs Island ferry start point and the departure times.
Time: Three to five hours.

···· *A few minutes after leaving Cable Wharf the ferry passes Georges Island and the South Terminal, both of which have played significant roles in the city's history.*

Georges Island

Early French explorers called this island "Il Ronde ou Raquette"—Snowshoe Island—for its shape. In 1745 the Duc D'Anville—commander of the ill-fated French expedition to recapture Louisbourg—was buried here, later to be reinterred at Louisbourg. When Cornwallis's expedition sailed into the harbour four years later, the transports first disembarked their passengers on the island—no doubt as a precaution against French and Indian attacks from the mainland forests.

Like a man o'war moored in the harbour just seaward of the original town, the small island was for 150 years the heart of the Halifax defences. Cornwallis immediately hit on it as "very convenient for a battery to defend both the harbour and the town" and within a year had built on it an earthwork fort mounting seven 32-pounder cannon.

Prince Edward's Star Fort (Straton, 1795).

During the American War of Independence the fort was enlarged to mount forty-eight cannon, and in 1794 Prince Edward transformed it into a "star fort" and named it **Fort Charlotte,** after the Queen. By the War of 1812 the fort had its own Martello tower and—supported by batteries on the town shore and on the Dartmouth side—it had become the main line of the harbour defences.

The present fort was constructed in the 1860s to mount rifled muzzle-loader guns; twelve 9-inch and 10-inch guns—protected by iron shields about 15 in. thick—were mounted in two levels of batteries with an elaborate underground magazine complex. By the turn of the century it had become the headquarters for a new form of warfare—submarine mining, the laying of mines in the harbour channel to prevent the entry of enemy ships. (The submarine mining establishment buildings may still be seen on the northeast side of the island.) During the First World War the island became the central anchor point for the submarine net strung across the harbour, protecting it with quick-firing guns. By the Second World War the island was no longer in military use.

···· *Directly opposite Georges Island on the Halifax side is the South Terminal.*

From 1761 on the town shoreline facing Georges Island stood the Grand Battery, which—together with Fort Charlotte on the island and Fort Clarence on the Dartmouth shore (situated where the oil tank farm is now)—for over a century made up the main line of the harbour defences.

During the Second World War, hundreds of thousands of Canadian servicemen travelling to the battlefields of Europe left from the tightly guarded quays and wharves of the **South Terminal.** Facing the harbour is the long Quay Wall, completed in 1931 and the berth of such legendary ships as *Queen Mary, Queen Elizabeth, Aquitania,* and the *Empress of Britain,* as well as the many Polish, Dutch, and French ships involved in the Allied effort during the Second World War. Leaving from this berth, the 85,000 ton *Queen Elizabeth,* stripped bare of her luxurious interior, carried 15,000 troops at a time and regularly used her great speed to elude the U-boat packs waiting in the Atlantic.

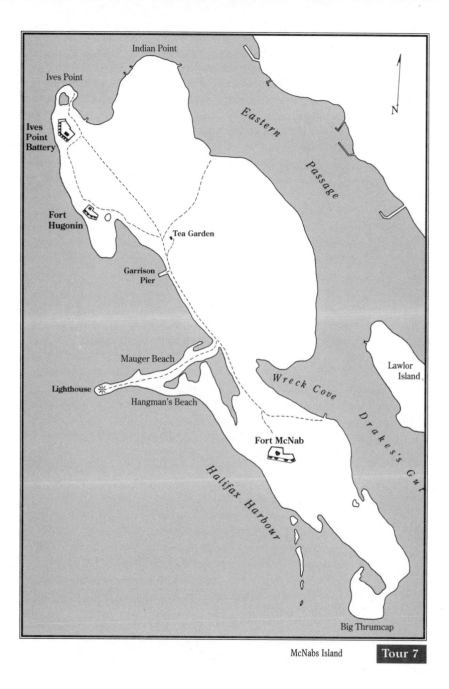

Indian Point

Ives Point

Ives Point Battery

Eastern Passage

N

Fort Hugonin

• Tea Garden

Garrison Pier

Mauger Beach

Lighthouse ☀

Hangman's Beach

Lawlor Island

Wreck Cove

Drake's Gut

Fort McNab

Halifax Harbour

Big Thrumcap

McNabs Island

Tour 7

McNabs Island

···· *On your first outing, the recommended tour is the southern part of the island, including Mauger Beach, Fort McNab, and Wreck Cove. Energetic hikers might want to go on to explore the northern part, including Ives Point.*

Southern Tour

···· *From Garrison Pier, turn right onto the gravel road and continue towards the turn-off for the beach.*

On the right a short distance along the road are the ruins of a concrete building, built during the Second World War to house pumps that forced oil from tankers moored at Garrison Pier to a large tank a few metres to the east of the building. It was protected by an anti-aircraft gun mounted on the roof.

Mauger Beach

This innocuous crescent of beach has been associated with some of Halifax's earliest history—and some of its grisliest.

Here, in 1698, the French set up their fishing station; situated close to the harbour entrance, the beach was ideal for drying their catch. Near the old station they proposed to build their town; it was to be guarded by a battery on the high bluffs on the opposite side of the harbour channel, on the exact spot where York Redoubt is now. In 1745 D'Anville's ships sailed past the island, discarding the bodies of dead crewmen, many of which were washed up on the beach; when, four years later, the British arrived, they named it Dead Man's Beach.

Within a few years of Halifax's founding, Joshua Mauger had acquired the beach that bears his name. He had made his start in the West Indies slave trade and in 1745 landed with the conquering troops in Louisbourg in time to share in the booty from the fortress's fall. When the garrison was transferred to Halifax, Mauger accompanied them. Within a few years he held the office of Agent Victualler to His Majesty's navy, indulging in a little privateering on the side.

From 1752 he ostensibly used the beach for a fishing station, but it seems likelier that he used the buildings—and the island's convenient coves and beaches—for rum smuggling (to, among others, the French in the reinstated Louisbourg fortress). His illicit dealings became too much for the Governor, and in 1761

Mauger returned to England; the following year he secured a seat in the British Parliament. He had one child who became the beautiful wife of a French nobleman close to Louis XVI; they were both beheaded during the French Revolution, and Joseph Mauger died shortly thereafter.

Between 1793 and 1809 the Royal Navy used the beach in the vicinity of the current lighthouse for gibbets to display the tarred bodies of its executed mutineers and deserters, to deter other seamen from similar actions.

Command of the sea between the island and York Redoubt was always crucial to the harbour's defence. On the site of the

WILDLIFE ON THE ISLAND

*T*he island is endowed with over 100 species of birds and waterfowl and more than 150 varieties of flowers, trees, and shrubs, many of them brought in by the early settlers. Following is a selection of some species seen on the island.

Birds: cormorants, Ospreys, Great Blue Herons, Red-tailed Hawks, "Pigeon" Hawks, "Sparrow" Hawks, hummingbirds, kingfishers, woodpeckers, warblers, several varieties of ducks, cuckoos, shrikes, swifts, swallows, jays, chickadees, plovers, and sandpipers.

Vegetation: blackberries, raspberries, roses, holly, lilies, lupines, English hawthorn, lilacs, queen-of-the-meadow, spruce, birch, Sugar Maple, beech, varieties of ferns and mosses.

There is also a variety of **animals,** including several fish species in the ponds and lagoon, such as sticklebacks, mummichugs, and American eels, as well as Red-backed Salamanders, Garter Snakes, and Red-bellied Snakes. Although sightings of other animals are rare, raccoons, bobcats, white-tailed deer, foxes, and rabbits have been seen on the island.

current lighthouse, in 1814 the British began construction of a stone Martello tower—**Sherbrooke Tower**—in the hope of controlling the sea channel; constructed of granite, it was three storeys high and was designed to mount seven guns. Against the advice of Colonel Gustavus Nicholls (the Citadel's architect), the Lieutenant-Governor of the time insisted on the tower's construction: he argued that its guns would indeed harass enemy ships in the channel and also bring fire into the sea under York Redoubt where the latter's guns couldn't reach—somehow overlooking the fact that the short range of smooth-bore cannon made both of these aims unrealistic. When finally completed in 1828 it had a lighthouse built on top and served in this useful function for some years.

Sherbrooke
Tower on
Mauger Beach
(Toles, 1815).

A few hundred metres along the south shoreline of the beach, just below the spit, are the **Strawberry Battery** ruins. This small Second World War battery was armed with two 12-pounder quick-firing guns supported by four searchlights, designed to cover the antisubmarine net strung between the lighthouse and York Redoubt.

···· *Return to the road and continue southwards.*

To your right is the lagoon. In the early 1800s it was open to the sea, and Peter McNab would have sailed from the harbour to the jetty near his house, located at the lagoon's southern end; at that time the area on the road side (east) of the lagoon was cultivated farmland.

···· *At the fork in the road at the top of the incline, turn right towards Fort McNab. On the right, just before you reach the old concrete barracks building on the left, is a path leading to the McNab family graveyard.*

The graveyard contains the remains of several generations of McNabs, as well as of servants of the family—marked by the wooden crosses—and of other families on the island. The fort was carefully constructed around the old stones, which made it, as Thomas Raddall has said, probably the best-guarded graveyard in the world.

Fort McNab

When completed in 1892 the fort was the furthest seaward and the most important of the harbour defences. Its cost was calculated as £24,000, supplied by some of the lavish profits of the imperially controlled Suez Canal.

Constructed of concrete-bearing heavy earth parapets, the fort originally mounted two 6-inch and one 10-inch breech-loading guns. (The latter weapon—the largest breech-loader ever mounted in Halifax—is now on display at York Redoubt.) In 1914 the fort was augmented by searchlights and became the examination battery, checking incoming ships. In the Second World War, activity centred on the Radar Tower and the associated plotting room.

As you approach the fort's casemates, follow the road to the right, up to the **gun emplacements.** Numbers 1 and 2 Gun Emplacements (the numbering is from right to left as you face seawards) were modified in 1914 to mount 6-inch guns; as late as 1954. Number 2 Emplacement was armed with a 4-inch gun. Number 3 Emplacement dates from the original construction of 1889-92. The tall (leftmost) structure was built over the original Number 4 Emplacement—as a **Radar Tower** during the Second World War. Beneath the ramparts are the magazines and gun

ESCAPE OF THE TALLAHASSEE

*F*rom the conflict's beginning in 1861, Nova Scotians were passionately involved in the United States Civil War. There was much sympathy for the North, with thousands of Nova Scotians enlisting on the Union side, including Joseph Howe's son. Until the First World War no other conflict was to claim the lives of so many Nova Scotians.

Halifax itself sided with the South. Some of its leading citizens were busy with the new industry of blockade-running, making huge profits on cargoes run past the Union warships into Southern ports. As thousands of Nova Scotians trooped off to fight the Confederacy, its agents swarmed over the capital, gathering supplies for the cause, copiously dispensing champagne, and Confederate currency. As if all this was not ironic enough, fear of American intentions accelerated work on the fortress, and several powerful forts were constructed during this period.

There were good reasons for the anxiety. First, a Union warship fired on the Royal Mail steamer *Trent* and forcibly removed some Confederate emissaries on their way to Britain; war between the two long-time adversaries was only narrowly averted. Then, in Nova Scotian waters, a Union cruiser seized the steamer *Chesapeake,* which had previously been hijacked by Confederate officers. When the ship was brought into Halifax for adjudication, some leading citizens arranged a fight on the waterfront, under cover of which the three Confederate officers made their escape from Northern wrath, eventually making their way back to Dixie. In the court battle over the *Chesapeake,* the judge decided that the ship should be returned to its Northern owners and was noisily abused in the Halifax Club as a result.

With these bits of derring-do, the war had spilled into Halifax. Probably the most famous—and, for Haligonians, the most exciting—of these high-seas adventures was the affair of the *Tallahassee,* a Southern raider that had sunk fifty Northern vessels before it was chased into Halifax by Union warships. Under the British neutrality laws the *Tallahassee* had exactly forty-eight hours to resupply, repair damage, and leave the harbour.

As many as thirteen Union cruisers gathered at the harbour mouth, while the Union gun-boat *Pontoosuck* waited off York Redoubt. The *Tallahassee*'s chances looked bleak. Haligonians watched tensely: among the many personal ties involved was the warm friendship of the *Tallahassee*'s Captain Wood with Admiral Hope of the station's British naval squadron.

Then, in the dead of night, led by a small boat taking soundings, a local pilot took the raider out the shallow Eastern Passage, using the ship's two propellers alternately to twist its way through the shoals. She gained the open sea and steamed away, leaving the Union warships watching vigilantly at the harbour mouth.

The personal ties proved strong. After the war Captain Wood, along with a number of unrepentant Confederate "rebels," settled in Halifax, their Southern courtesy gracing the city's social life for years to come.

....

crews' shelters: the building next to the roadway behind Number 2 Emplacement is a shelter for crews of the 6-inch guns. The low structure behind and overlooking the emplacements is the **Battery Command Post,** constructed during the Second World War.

From the ramparts or from the Radar Tower there is a vivid sense of the fort's role: with its powerful guns capable of reaching targets miles out to sea, it was designed—in cooperation with Sandwich Battery (just south of York Redoubt, visible on the bluffs on the far side of the sea channel)—to command the harbour mouth and the entire harbour approaches from Chebucto Head to Cole Harbour, as well as covering the coastline between Chebucto Head and York Redoubt.

At the most seaward point of the island is **Big Thrumcap.** In the late 1700s Peter McNab's shepherd made his home on this barren and exposed spit of land. The whitecaps and breakers around Big Thrumcap mark the location of the shoals, which over the years have claimed many ships and seamen as they steered towards the harbour entrance. The most famous and tragic wreck, with great loss of life, was of HMS *La Tribune* in 1797.

···· *From Fort McNab return to the main road and take the fork to Wreck Cove.*

Wreck Cove is a pleasant and secluded stretch of beach and wooded glades, well suited for picnicking or a rest stop. The cove gains its name from the wrecked vessels that drifted or were dumped here. Opposite the cove is Lawlor Island, situated in the shallow Eastern Passage to the harbour. In 1711 the French planned a fort for the island to guard the channel and to protect their envisaged town on McNabs Island. It was down this channel that, during the American Civil War, the Confederate raider *Tallahassee* made her daring escape from the Union warships.

From the 1870s **Lawlor Island** was used by the Sisters of Charity to care for shipborne victims of contagious diseases, who were not permitted to land in Halifax; all ships flying the yellow flag indicating disease on board were directed to the island. The ruins of the dock and several small structures are all that remain of the quarantine hospital.

···· *This concludes the tour of the southern part of the island. Take the gravel road to return to the Island Tea Garden and Garrison Pier area.*

Northern Tour

As the site of intensely popular nineteenth-century recreation grounds, the northern part of the island may have seen the most fervent human activity over the years; these old playgrounds have, however, largely been reclaimed by nature. The area also contains two semi-ruined sea batteries, one of which—Ives Point Battery—may be visited.

···· *From the Garrison Pier or Island Tea Garden, walk northwards along the gravel road until it intersects with the Old Military Road (now a fairly overgrown broad path); turn right on the Old Military Road and continue up the hill.*

Several hundred metres along the road, a path branches off to the left. Once called Carousel Road, it led to Finlay's Picnic Grounds, a highly popular resort in the first years of this century that offered a large open-air dance hall, a merry-go-round, and a large number of games stalls. An area half-overgrown by shrubs is all that remains today.

A track runs from the Old Military Road down to the beach. A few minutes' walk further along the road, past the track, brings you to the area once occupied by Woolnough's Picnic Grounds. These were opened in 1873 and catered to hundreds of people at a time; ferried across the harbour by steamers and an array of other vessels, they spent exuberant days dancing in the pavilion, playing football and quoits, or simply strolling on the tree-shaded lawns. Today little can be seen of the original grounds.

···· *Continuing along the road brings you to Ives Point Battery.*

Ives Point Battery

Built between 1865 and 1870 amid fears of conflict with the United States during and after the American Civil War, this sea battery was designed for the powerful new rifled guns. Its role was to cooperate with the Point Pleasant batteries in the defence of the sea channel leading to the inner harbour.

The battery was armed with heavy weapons—six 9-inch and three 10-inch rifled muzzle-loaders—all originally protected by thick iron shields. The 9-inch guns crossed fire with Fort Ogilvie on Point Pleasant, while the 10-inch guns faced seaward and could fire towards York Redoubt. Two of the 10-inch guns may be seen, still mounted in the southernmost emplacements, while a further seven guns lie in the shrubbery on the edge of the parade ground.

These old weapons, built at the full flush of history's most sweeping empire, almost glow with a sense of the past, bearing as they do the initials of the Queen-Empress and—across six hundred years—the chivalric ideals of an English King. The cypher on the gun barrels, VR (Victoria Regina), is surrounded by the famous motto of the British monarchy, *Honi Soit Qui Mal Y Pense*—"Dishonour To Him Who Thinks Ill Of This." The motto is inscribed on a garter. In 1348, Edward III, obsessed by the ideals of chivalry, founded the Order of the Garter to embody the ideals of the Knights of the Round Table; the original garter was said to

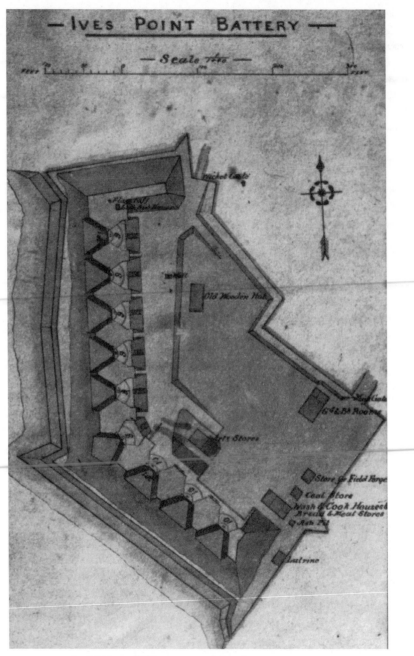

Ives Point Battery (1877).

have dropped from the leg of the "Fair Lady of Kent" at a ball, whereupon the King picked it up, tied it round his own leg, and uttered the famous motto.

In the 1890s a concrete reconstruction was begun at the battery's northern end for breech-loading weapons, when two 6-inch and two 12-pounder quick-firing guns were mounted. In the First World War searchlights were added to assist in the battery's coverage of the antisubmarine net and minefield between Ives Point and Point Pleasant. By the Second World War the harbour defences had shifted seawards, and the battery was no longer useful.

From Ives Point Battery the road curves down to the water at **Ives Point,** named for Captain Benjamin Ives, an officer in the brilliantly successful New England expedition against the Fortress of Louisbourg in 1745. In the nineteenth century, the point was served by a wharf used to land men, equipment, and supplies for the Ives Point Battery and Fort Hugonin.

The more adventurous explorer—and one with a few extra hours to spare—can hike from Ives Point beach (next to Ives Point) to **Indian Point** at the northern tip of the island. From here the Micmac may have launched raids against the new settlements of Halifax and Dartmouth, and from 1762—after the English had gained dominance over the Indians' French allies— the Micmac peacably camped here for many years.

···· *To return from the Ives Point area to the Island Tea Garden and Garrison Pier area, take either the Old Military Road or the gravel road (a slightly longer route).*

At the pointed metal picket fence, the gravel road passes **Fort Hugonin,** which is on Department of National Defence Property and off limits to the public. The fort was built in 1899 as a rapid-fire defence to prevent the entry of fast torpedo boats into the harbour and also to cover the inadequately defended shore near the foot of York Redoubt; it was armed with four 12-pounder quick-firing guns. Manned and armed during the First World War, it was not used during the next war.

References

Further Reading

Bird, Michael J. 1995. *The Town That Died*. Toronto: McGraw-Hill
    Ryerson, 1962. Reprint, Halifax: Nimbus Publishing Ltd.

Comiter, Alvin, and Elizabeth Pacey. 1988. *Historic Halifax*. Willowdale,
    ON: Hounslow Press.

Pacey, Elizabeth. 1987. *Georgian Halifax*. Hantsport, NS: Lancelot Press.

Raddall, Thomas H. 1993. *Halifax: Warden of the North*. Halifax: Nimbus.

Selected References

The following sources, used in the preparation of the guide, can be found
in bookstores, libraries, or the Public Archives of Nova Scotia.

Africville Genealogy Society, eds. 1992. *The Spirit of Africville*. Halifax:
    Formac Publishing Co.

Akins, T. B. 1973. *History of Halifax City.* Nova Scotia Historical Society,
    1895. Facsimile Edition, Belleville, ON: Mika Publishing.

Bird, Michael J. 1995. *The Town That Died*. Toronto: McGraw-Hill
    Ryerson. 1962. Reprint, Halifax: Nimbus Publishing Ltd.

Borrett, Wm. C. 1944. *East Coast Port and Other Tales Told Under the Old
    Town Clock*. Halifax: Imperial Publishing Co.

Collins, Louis W. 1975. *In Halifax Town*. Halifax: Halcraft Printing.

Comiter, Alvin, and Elizabeth Pacey. 1988. *Historic Halifax*. Willowdale,
    ON: Hounslow Press.

Erikson, Paul A. 1986. *Halifax's North End*. Hantsport, NS: Lancelot Press.

Greenough, John Joseph. 1977. *The Halifax Citadel 1825–60: A Narrative
    and Structural History*. Canadian Historical Sites No. 17, Ottawa: Parks
    Canada.

Heine, Wm. C. 1987. *96 Years in the Royal Navy*. Hantsport, NS: Lancelot
    Press.

Heritage Trust of Nova Scotia. 1967. *Founded Upon A Rock*. Heritage Trust
    of Nova Scotia.

Hill, Kay. 1980. *Joe Howe: The Man Who was Nova Scotia*. Toronto:
    McClelland and Stewart.

Johnston, A. J. B. 1981. *Defending Halifax: Ordnance 1825–1906*. History
    and Archeology No. 46, Ottawa: Parks Canada.

Metson, Graham. 1981. *An East Coast Port*. Toronto: McGraw-Hill Ryerson.

———, ed. 1978. *The Halifax Explosion: December 6, 1917*. Toronto:
    McGraw-Hill Ryerson.

Morris, James. 1968. *Pax Britannica: The Climax of an Empire*. New York:
    Harcourt, Brace & World.

Morrison, James H. 1982. *Wave to Whisper: British Military Communications in Halifax and the Empire, 1780–1880.* History and Archeology No. 64., Ottawa: Parks Canada.

Pacey, Elizabeth. 1987. *Georgian Halifax.* Hantsport, NS: Lancelot Press.

Piers, Harry. 1947. *The Evolution of the Halifax Fortress 1749–1928.* Revised by G. M. Self and Phyllis Blakeley, Public Archives of Nova Scotia, Publication No. 7.

Redman, Stanley R. 1981. *Open Gangway.* Hantsport, NS: Lancelot Press.

Smith, Marilyn Gurney. *1985. The King's Yard: An Illustrated History of the Halifax Dockyard.* Halifax: Nimbus Publishing Ltd.

Stacey, Col. C. P. 1949. *Halifax as an International Strategic Factor 1749–1949.* Annual Report of the Canadian Historical Association.

Whitehead, Ruth Holmes 1991. *The Old Man Told Us: Excerpts from Micmac History 1500–1950.* Halifax: Nimbus Publishing Ltd.

Whitfield, Carol M. 1981. *Tommy Atkins: The British Soldier in Canada, 1759–1870.* History and Archeology No. 56, Ottawa: Parks Canada.

Index